BURLINGTON CHRISTIAN FELLOWSHIP
2054 Mountainside Drive
Burlington, ON L7P 1A8

Secret Heroine of the Bible

Getting Back Up After a Devastating Hit

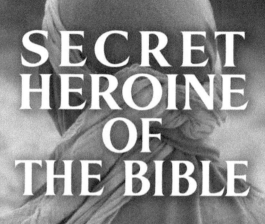

SECRET HEROINE OF THE BIBLE

Getting Back Up After A Devastating Hit

RICHARD CIARAMITARO

Belleville, Ontario, Canada

SECRET HEROINE OF THE BIBLE
Copyright © 2021, Richard Ciaramitaro

All Rights Reserved. No part of this publication may be reproduced, stored in a retrieval system or transmitted in any form or by any means—electronic, mechanical, photocopy, recording or any other—except for brief quotations in printed reviews, without the prior permission of the author.

All Scripture quotations, unless otherwise specified, are from *The Holy Bible, New King James Version.* Copyright © 1979, 1980, 1982. Thomas Nelson Inc., Publishers. • Scriptures marked KJV are from *The Holy Bible, King James Version.* Copyright © 1977, 1984, Thomas Nelson Inc., Publishers. • Scriptures marked NLT are taken from *The Holy Bible, New Living Translation.* Copyright © 1996, 2004, 2007, 2013, 2015 by Tyndale House Foundation. Used by permission of Tyndale House Publishers, Inc., Carol Stream, Illinois 60188. All rights reserved.

Cataloguing data available from Library and Archives Canada

ISBN: 978-1-4600-1303-8
LSI Edition: 978-1-4600-1304-5
E-book ISBN: 978-1-4600-1305-2

(E-book available from the Kindle Store, KOBO and the iBooks Store)

To order additional copies, visit:
www.essencebookstore.com

Guardian Books is an imprint of *Essence Publishing,* a Christian Book Publisher dedicated to furthering the work of Christ through the written word. For more information, contact:
20 Hanna Court, Belleville, Ontario, Canada K8P 5J2
Phone: 1-800-238-6376 • Fax: (613) 962-3055
Email: info@essence-publishing.com
Web site: www.essence-publishing.com

Table of Contents

Introduction 7

1. The Family Life of Job 13

2. Behind the Scenes of Spiritual Warfare 33

3. The Pain in the Storm. 47

4. Digging Out of the Ashes 63

5. Job's Wife 83

6. Jeremiah—One Day at a Time. 95

7. Keziah—A Sweet Aroma 103

8. Keren-Happuch—Rise Up and Be Restored 111

Introduction

In my book, *The Secret of the Kingdom of Life,* I shared how thanksgiving is the "secret" to operating in Kingdom life and obtaining breakthroughs in our journey of faith. In this book, *Job's Wife: the Secret Heroine of the Bible,* I share a revelation of biblical restoration concerning Job's wife that is a simple "secret" of Scripture, yet profound.

In life, and in the Bible, we often hear about the heroes or heroines of faith and some of the incredible tests they faced against impossible odds. With opposition on every side, they kept going, in spite of setbacks, disappointments, betrayals, and failures. Even when they missed the mark, or experienced hurts and pain, they persevered to become biblical heroes. King David was one of them.

Hunted down and treated like a wild animal by King Saul for seventeen years, David persevered to become Israel's greatest King. His family rejected him, his brothers looked down upon him and even mocked him, yet he wrote Psalm 23, saying, *"He restoreth my soul."* Later David committed adultery with Bathsheba. When she became pregnant, he put out a hit on her husband and had him killed. The son Bathsheba carried—King David's son—died.

Could things get worse? Yes! David's son Amnon committed incest with his sister. His brother Absalom killed him, rebelled against his father, and tried to usurp his throne. Yet David prevailed.

In the Book of Ruth we also see Naomi, whose name means "sweet" or "pleasant," yet her life was anything but sweet and pleasant for many years—a contradiction that often comes before breakthrough. Naomi married a man named Elimelech and they lived in Bethlehem. They had two sons—Mahlon and Chilion. When a serious famine hit Judea, the family moved to Moab, and the two sons married Moabite women—Orpah and Ruth.

Things were great for about ten years, but then tragedy hit and the husband, Elimelech, died. Shortly after his death both Naomi's sons died. Now three widows suffered sadness, grief, pain, and incredible loss. When the famine ended, Naomi decided to move back to Bethlehem. Ruth, who went with her, married Boaz and had a son who they named Obed. Obed became David's grandfather and an ancestor of Jesus Christ. The story is powerful because it shows the restoring power of God, who can take a broken heart and unspeakable loss, and create good out of the most overwhelming circumstances. Since Naomi prevailed in these circumstances, she is truly a heroine—a woman of incredible courage and strength, and she earned a reputation for her heroic deeds and compassionate character. These characteristics are a true reflection of her life.

Many brave women today display these qualities. I have seen some of them. They came from abused backgrounds and were on the streets stuck in addictions. Wounded, devastated, hopeless, rejected, soliciting men, and written off by many, they entered the Windsor Life Centre (WLC)—a treatment home for women struggling with addictions in Windsor, Ontario, Canada. In WLC they found hope through the program again and again, over a period of six months to a year. They regained dignity, recovered their dreams, and some even regained their families and children. God graciously restored their lives.

Day by day, week by week, and month by month the process of restoration took place in the lives of these precious women. They rose up, entered the workforce with new joy, went back to school, and excelled; some got married and had children. They made something good of their lives, and moved forward out of the ruts and setbacks of their past into a new future, with God as the centre of their lives.

These are the heroines of our day—knocked down in life, but not knocked out; formerly shamed, but now in God's "Hall of Fame," just like Rahab, the prostitute in the Bible, whom God took out of the "Hall of Shame" and placed into the "Hall of Fame" described in Hebrews 11.

"For a righteous man may fall seven times and rise again, but the wicked shall fall by calamity. Do not rejoice when your enemy falls, and do not let your heart be glad when he stumbles" (Proverbs 24:16-17).

The true heroines and heroes of the Bible were men and women who took a fall, but got back up again, achieved greatness in their lives and broke the patterns of failure off of generations to come.

This book is about getting back up again after a terrible devastation has hit your life. It is about allowing the Holy Spirit to restore you—a work of grace and mercy from a restoring God.

"The Lord is my shepherd; I shall not want. He makes me to lie down in green pastures; He leads me beside the still waters. He restores my soul; He leads me in the paths of righteousness for His name's sake" (Psalm 23:1-3).

In my first book, *The Five Tests of Faith*, I portrayed Job's wife wrongly as not a very nice person—a loser and miserable failure. But in this book, she is truly a heroine—a woman of distinguished courage or ability, admired for her brave deeds and noble qualities. She is none other than *Job's Wife: Secret Heroine of the Bible!*

I have learned to be very careful not to make blanket judgments and demeaning statements about people because of the mess-ups and consequences they might be suffering, and I have especially learned never to write anyone off. Our God is a Champion at taking devastated, broken lives and restoring them. As the psalmist David said, *"He restores my soul."* Restore here means "to be re-established or bring back home again." God wants to re-establish our lives and bring us back home again.

Maybe you are that person who others have written off.

Maybe you have failed time and time again.

Maybe through this book the Holy Spirit will touch your heart and bring hope back into your soul. My friend, God is much more merciful than the most merciful people I know, and He wants you back into relationship with Him: *"For You, Lord, are good, and ready to forgive, and abundant in mercy to all those who call upon You. Give ear, O LORD, to my prayer; and attend to the voice of my supplications"* (Psalm 86:5-6).

Please hear me, my friend: "God is abundant in mercy." It's not too late! Again, it's not too late! Read through these pages and watch your life return. God is not done with your life my friend; the Enemy of our souls says differently, but trust in God's abundant mercy today.

CHAPTER ONE

The Family Life of Job

"There was a man in the land of Uz, whose name was Job; and that man was blameless and upright, and one who feared God and shunned evil. And seven sons and three daughters were born to him. Also, his possessions were seven thousand sheep, three thousand camels, five hundred yoke of oxen, five hundred female donkeys, and a very large household, so that this man was the greatest of all the people of the East. And his sons would go and feast in their houses, each on his appointed day, and would send and invite their three sisters to eat and drink with them. So it was, when the days of feasting had run their course, that Job would send and sanctify them, and he would rise early in the morning and offer burnt offerings according to the number of them all. For Job said, 'It may be that my sons have sinned and cursed God in their hearts.' Thus Job did regularly" (Job 1:1-5).

[INTRO:] Certain characteristics accompany men who

are blessed of the Lord with prosperity in the material realm. The beginning of the Book of Job introduces the incredible story of one such man—Job, a blessed man. Some characteristics of a man blessed of the Lord with wealth are: a happy marriage, many children, and blessed beyond measure.

> *"I love those who love me, and those who seek me diligently will find me. Riches and honor are with me, enduring riches and righteousness. My fruit is better than gold, yes, than fine gold, and my revenue than choice silver. I traverse the way of righteousness, in the midst of the paths of justice, that I may cause those who love me to inherit wealth, that I may fill their treasuries"* (Proverbs 8:17-21).

> *"In the house of the righteous there is much treasure, but in the revenue of the wicked is trouble"* (Proverbs 15:6).

> *"By humility and the fear of the LORD are riches and honor and life"* (Proverbs 22:4).

I have learned over these many years in ministry that God desires to have first place in our hearts, marriages, finances, and families. We never seek the riches, but we seek first the Kingdom of God and His righteousness, and all these things are given to us. God must be number one in our lives—that is Lordship.

It is easy to create a plausible portrait of Job through this observation. Assuming then, that Job had a good wife and good marriage, what might his family life have looked like?

In the natural, Job and his wife had everything going for them. He had become the richest person in the entire region where they dwelt. We can assume he and his wife had lands, houses, and servants, but we know for sure from Scripture that they had ten children.

Everybody would have known this family, and the children likely knew other children in the community. With Job's abundance of livestock and herds, they would have been known as well-to-do.

Oftentimes, many well-off people are confident as well as disciplined—two characteristics of many successful entrepreneurs today. Many well-off people I know are quite generous, and I am sure Job's family helped the less fortunate in their immediate community and surrounding region as well. They probably attended many community gatherings in their town and got to know their neighbours and fellow community members well.

Today many good and successful businessmen and business women are people who love to give back to their communities, because of their strong spirit of generosity and philanthropy that garners them a positive reputation in their communities. We can assume it would have been the same in Job's day.

Families who do well are also generally known to be optimistic and positive in their outlook. Couples are usually very committed to each other in their marriage relationships, and to their children. On weekends, I am sure, Job's family would have had meals together. Dad would have probably enjoyed activities and hobbies, such as building things and taking on new projects with his seven sons. They had enough people in their family for an entire baseball team, if you included Mom and Dad.

I imagine Job and his wife would have had a joyful and fulfilling time raising their seven boys. The boys and their parents were probably closely knit together in relationship, and very likely many new business ventures developed through family gatherings and times of sharing. Eventually, some of them may have helped Dad take care of the family businesses that had become increasingly prosperous, to include seven thousand sheep, three thousand camels, five hundred yoke of oxen, and five hundred female donkeys. Their many servants, chefs, porters, and cleaners who worked in various guest quarters, all may have lived together in the same house.

Not only was the couple blessed with seven sons, but they also had daughters—the pride and joy of Dad and Mom. We can picture them as being very beautiful, friendly, and kind, with an entrepreneurial spirit, as many of the children of successful entrepreneurs are today. Their mother probably taught them etiquette and how to dress in the latest fashion of the day. As young ladies of high social standing, they could have been fashion leaders in their school and town, but they also would have learned domestic skills—how to select the best foods, and how to cook exquisite meals in a house with a huge kitchen and many gadgets. They would have learned from their mother how to start their own businesses, raise children, and enjoy frequent times of fellowship with the family. These are some of the things many well-off people often do, and that is a common lifestyle they could have embraced.

The Book of Job tells us Job's character was blameless, which speaks of a man who lacks nothing in physical strength or beauty. He was a wholesome guy! What woman wouldn't want a man with integrity, high ethics, good morals, and abundant wealth? Job's wife was favoured of God to find him, but there is one more thing about her husband that Scripture reveals: Job feared God and stayed away from evil. What a guy! A few of the blessings associated with folks that fear the Lord are mentioned in the Psalms and Proverbs.

> *"Behold, the eye of the LORD is on those who fear Him, on those who hope in His mercy, to deliver their soul from death, and to keep them alive in famine"* (Psalm 33:18-19).

> *"The angel of the LORD encampeth round about them that fear Him, and delivereth them. O taste and see that the LORD is good: blessed is the man that trusteth in Him. O fear the LORD, ye His saints: for there is no want to them that fear Him"* (Psalm 34:7-9, KJV).

> *"He who despises the word will be destroyed, but he who fears the commandment will be rewarded"* (Proverbs 13:13).

> *"In the fear of the LORD is strong confidence: and His children shall have a place of refuge. The fear of the LORD is a fountain of life, to depart from the snares of death"* (Proverbs 14:26-27, KJV).

These are just a few of hundreds of Scriptures referencing blessings the fear of the Lord bestows on our lives. Job had them all going for him. I believe this fear of the Lord was very attractive to Job's wife, and was a characteristic that she admired in her husband.

This man feared God and stayed away from evil. He wasn't a womanizer. He was faithful and loyal to God and to his wife. There was nothing shady about him. He was faithful in his business dealings and a man of highest ethics and character. He was trustworthy, honest, dedicated, and morally upright. He and his wife were probably one happy couple—so in love, so connected, so together that they probably were just as madly in love with one another as I am with my wife Cathy; just as excited to meet at the door when he came home from work; just as full of joy to hang out with each other.

Holidays must have been the best ever for the two of them. When all their children moved out, possibly to get married, they became empty nesters, but trouble was brewing. Their sons loved to party. They feasted and invited their sisters to join them. Like a good and virtuous father, it was Job's regular practice to pray regularly for his kids. He wanted to see them walk in the ways of the Lord, but their banquets, with drinking and feasting, lasted for days at a time. Dad probably had many heart-to-heart talks with his sons to warn them, but was getting a bit worried that they might turn away from God.

Over a period of time the partying caught up with Job's children. It opened a door for the Enemy to enter, and for the hedge of protection around them to be removed, or lowered. Havoc and chaos resulted and devastated Job's family.

From my studies, I believe the open door that allows the Enemy of our soul, Satan, to enter us, is fear. Fear is the opposite of faith, and in Job 3:25-26 it says: *"For the thing I greatly feared has come upon me, and what I dreaded has happened to me. I am not at ease, nor am I quiet; I have no rest, for trouble comes."*

Greatly feared means "to be in alarm, terror, dread; to be in extreme apprehension of something in the future." In my short journey of faith these last forty-four years, I have recognized that fear is a spirit: *"For God has not given us a spirit of fear, but of power and of love and of a sound mind"* (2 Timothy 1:7). I have seen many folks make bad decisions out of fear, without faith, and they paid a dear price.

Fear is insidious. It has a paralyzing element. It is contagious, and can spread quickly and easily if we are not walking in faith. Fear is detrimental to our spiritual health and must be resisted. Remember the story of the twelve spies in the book of Numbers, Chapters 12 and 13. Their fear of giants in the land spread to the Israelites and cost all those, twenty years and up, their lives—they died in the wilderness. We must stand up against fear and have it broken off our lives.

All of us have encountered fear. I sense that somebody reading this has been rooted in, and led by a spirit of fear to dig a huge pit for their life. Is that you? Repent of it today and get back in faith. Don't use the world's wisdom, or yield to the world's ways. Trust God, who is faithful, not fearful.

To somebody else who is reading—you are in a very bad, physically abusive relationship, and the only reason you have stayed in it is because of fear. My friend, reach out and get some help today. You are not meant to be a punching bag, nor are you meant to succumb to ongoing threats. There is help. Ask the Holy Spirit to show you who to connect with for help.

In my forty-four years of ministry, some of the greatest spiritual battles I have fought have been with fear: fear of failure, feelings at times of never measuring up, thoughts of not being good enough, fear of failing people, and fear of the unknown. Oftentimes people's expectations are much more than we bargained for. As Pastors, we can't be at every birthday party, retirement party, or anniversary. It's impossible, but fear speaks loudly and clearly during these times, through fear of failing God or disappointing people, or fear of trusting again after a betrayal. This type of fear can come upon a Pastor when key members leave his church. Fear asks, "How many people will go with them?"

Fear of rejection; fear of abandonment—these are all onslaughts against our minds, designed to destroy our faith. How do we handle these situations?

When fear comes against my mind, I speak God's Word to it and resist it. I oppose it. I don't meditate upon it. Look what Scripture says:

> *"Fear not, for I am with you; be not dismayed, for I am your God. I will strengthen you, Yes, I will help you, I will uphold you with My righteous right hand"* (Isaiah 41:10).

> *"The LORD is my light and my salvation; whom shall I fear? The LORD is the strength of my life; of whom shall I be afraid? When the wicked came against me to eat up my flesh, my enemies and foes, they stumbled and fell. Though an army may encamp against me, my heart shall not fear; though war may rise against me, in this I will be confident. One thing I have desired of the LORD, that will I seek: that I may dwell in the house of the LORD all the days of my life, to behold the beauty of the LORD, and to inquire in His temple. For in the time of trouble He shall hide me in His pavilion; in the secret place of His tabernacle He shall hide me; He shall set me high upon a rock"* (Psalm 27:1-5).

See fear as an enemy of faith. See fear as a fiery dart the Enemy is sending against your mind.

Destroy fear!
Resist fear!

Never make a decision based on fear, but rather on faith in God.

Fear, like any other temptation, must be resisted. Stand up against it! *"For you did not receive the spirit of bondage again to fear, but you received the Spirit of adoption by whom we cry out, 'Abba, Father'"* (Romans 8:15).

When fear is around, the Devil is right behind it. Scripture calls fear a "spirit." Goliath planted fear into the hearts of the Israelite army in the days of King Saul and paralyzed the army as a result of his daily challenges. Sanballat and Tobiah of Hezekiah's day were hired to sow fear in the people.

Job did the right thing in praying and sacrificing for his children, but he did it out of fear. I am convinced that fear destroys the hedge of protection around our lives, homes, marriages, and finances.

> *"Now there was a day when the sons of God came to present themselves before the LORD, and Satan also came among them. And the LORD said to Satan, 'From where do you come?' So Satan answered the Lord and said, 'From going to and fro on the earth, and from walking back and forth on it.' Then the LORD said to Satan, 'Have you considered My servant Job, that there is none like him on the earth, a blameless and upright man, one who fears God and shuns evil?' So Satan answered the LORD and said, 'Does Job fear God for nothing? Have You not made a hedge around him, around his household, and around all that he has on*

> *every side? You have blessed the work of his hands, and his possessions have increased in the land. But now, stretch out Your hand and touch all that he has, and he will surely curse You to Your face!' And the LORD said to Satan, 'Behold, all that he has is in your power; only do not lay a hand on his person.' So Satan went out from the presence of the LORD"* (Job 1:6-12).

First of all, here we see that Satan is a real person with a voice and a strategy, and that his work as adversary is to be a hater and opponent—an Enemy. This name is found fifty-four times in Scripture. Satan is the Accuser of the Brethren, always trying to bring an accusation, a charge, an offense, or a crime against us. He is a legalist, and incredibly shrewd, cunning, crafty, and deceptive. The Accuser wants to make you afraid, to mock and ridicule you, to wear you down with worry, and always to question your walk and dedication to the Lord. He delights in making people feel hopeless, and tells you it's too late for you to change; you will never change. Satan always zeroes in on getting us to doubt the character and integrity of God.

God is good, not bad.
God is Holy, not unclean.
God is Faithful, not untrustworthy.
God is a God of forgiveness, not bitterness.

The greatest revelation of truth that has kept me serving God over the years, has been getting to know the character of God. If you want to know what God is like, read the Gospels of Matthew, Mark, Luke, and John.

> *"Philip said to Him [Jesus], 'LORD, show us the Father, and it is sufficient for us.' Jesus said to him, 'Have I been with you so long, and yet you have not known Me,*

Philip? He who has seen Me has seen the Father; so how can you say, "Show us the Father"? Do you not believe that I am in the Father, and the Father in Me? The words that I speak to you I do not speak on My own authority; but the Father who dwells in Me does the works. Believe Me that I am in the Father and the Father in Me, or else believe Me for the sake of the works themselves'" (John 14:8-11).

Get that revelation inside of you! *"He who has seen Me has seen the Father."* Do you want to know what the Father God is like? Just look at His Son through the Gospels.

Now here is list of a few of Satan's works:

"God anointed Jesus of Nazareth with the Holy Spirit and with power, who went about doing good and healing all who were oppressed by the devil, for God was with Him" (Acts 10:38).

"So Satan went out from the presence of the LORD, and struck Job with painful boils from the sole of his foot to the crown of his head" (Job 2:7).

Here we see the one who brings sickness and disease is the adversary, not God.

"Then he showed me Joshua the high priest standing before the Angel of the LORD, and Satan standing at his right hand to oppose him" (Zechariah 3:1).

The one bringing opposition, criticism, resistance, combativeness, antagonism, or hostility against us is the Enemy. I am convinced that the critical spirit is right from the boardroom of hell, and that the human critics Satan uses, have yielded to that foul destructive spirit:

> *"If Satan casts out Satan, he is divided against himself. How then will his kingdom stand?"* (Matthew 12:26).

Kingdom is found 389 times in Scripture and means "the domain, or territory of a leader governed by a single ruler, or government." Satan is the King over his Kingdom. He has a structure in his government with principalities, powers, wicked spirits, rulers, and demons. They are directly opposed to the purposes of the Kingdom of Heaven and mercilessly attack the ambassadors of the Kingdom—you and me today: *"Then Satan entered Judas, surnamed Iscariot, who was numbered among the twelve"* (Luke 22:3).

The Devil wants to get into our heads first. Satan starts his evil work by planting a thought into our minds. If we then ponder on that thought long enough, it becomes a stronghold in our mind. Over time if we allow or permit Satan in our minds and thinking, this opens the door to his oppression. An example would be someone getting offended like Judas did over Mary's expensive perfume being used on Jesus. Judas was upset, meditated on his upset, and it got into his soul over time. Bitterness, unforgiveness, and jealousy are all entry points Satan uses to inflict our minds and souls. Then he attacks and weakens our hearts. That's why it's so important to "guard" our hearts from bitterness, resentments, grudges, unforgiveness, betrayals, and hurts.

> *"But Peter said, 'Ananias, why has Satan filled your heart to lie to the Holy Spirit and keep back part of the price of the land for yourself?'"* (Acts 5:3).

> *"...to open their eyes, in order to turn them from darkness to light, and from the power of Satan to God, that they*

The Family Life of Job   25

may receive forgiveness of sins and an inheritance among those who are sanctified by faith in Me'" (Acts 26:18).

These are just a few of the works of the Enemy of our soul—the Devil, or Satan. His character is evil. His hatred for God and his people is wicked. His works are destructive and can be summarized with the words from John 10:10:

"The thief does not come except to steal, and to kill, and to destroy. I have come that they may have life, and that they may have it more abundantly."

After the Accuser of the Brethren left Heaven, he came to earth to cause havoc for Job, his wife, and their family, to destroy their lives and their livelihood. This passage describes how Job loses his property and his children:

"Now there was a day when his sons and daughters were eating and drinking wine in their oldest brother's house; and a messenger came to Job and said, 'The oxen were plowing and the donkeys feeding beside them, when the Sabeans raided them and took them away—indeed they have killed the servants with the edge of the sword; and I alone have escaped to tell you!' While he was still speaking, another also came and said, 'The fire of God fell from heaven and burned up the sheep and the servants, and consumed them; and I alone have escaped to tell you!' While he was still speaking, another also came and said, 'The Chaldeans formed three bands, raided the camels and took them away, yes, and killed the servants with the edge of the sword; and I alone have escaped to tell you!' While he was still speaking, another also came and said, 'Your sons and daughters were eating and drinking wine in their oldest brother's house,

and suddenly a great wind came from across the wilderness and struck the four corners of the house, and it fell on the young people, and they are dead; and I alone have escaped to tell you!' Then Job arose, tore his robe, and shaved his head; and he fell to the ground and worshiped. And he said: 'Naked I came from my mother's womb, and naked shall I return there. The LORD gave, and the LORD has taken away; blessed be the name of the LORD.' In all this Job did not sin nor charge God with wrong" (Job 1:13-22).

Everything changed in a moment of time: Job lost his family, his property, his livelihood. All was destroyed. He lost his sheep and the servants who had so faithfully served him. He lost his camels, and the servants tending them were killed by the invaders with a sword. A whirlwind, or tornado of some kind came, and all ten of his children died. Tragedy hit on every front for Job and his wife. The pain was unbearable; the suffering of losing everything in a moment of time, tragic and overwhelming.

Fifteen years ago, my wife lost her younger sister, Jennifer, to a brain tumor. I will never forget the day we arrived at the Fort Lauderdale port. As soon as we disembarked from the cruise ship, Cathy called home only to find out that her sister had passed away. It was a very sad funeral, and the family was wrecked from their loss. Can you imagine for just one moment what it would have been like to lose not just one child in a tragic accident, but to lose all ten in one day? The pain the parents experienced would have been indescribable. On top of that, their livelihood and business were also destroyed overnight. What would it be like if everything you had worked for all your life was suddenly taken from you?

Job, when he learned of these disasters, made a statement we have come to know as one of the most famous and frequently quoted passages of Scripture:

> *"And he said: "Naked I came from my mother's womb, and naked shall I return there. The LORD gave, and the LORD has taken away; blessed be the name of the LORD"* (Job 1:21).

These were Job's words, but it is not a statement of truth. He spoke them in the bitterness of his heart from the grief, pain, and loss he was experiencing; but it didn't end there. This was just the beginning of tragedy for Job and his wife.

Bear with me, because now I want to tell you about the secret heroine of the Bible—Job's wife!

If it wasn't enough for Job and his wife to lose their children and livelihood, and not understand why; not understand who was behind the destruction; not understand the work of the Enemy in the spiritual realm, that is much more real than the natural realm and world we live in; now the Enemy of Job and God had another strategy to get Job to deny the Lord. Satan would hit his health and marriage.

See how Satan attacks Job's health:

> *"Again there was a day when the sons of God came to present themselves before the LORD, and Satan came also among them to present himself before the LORD. And the LORD said to Satan, 'From where do you come?' Satan answered the LORD and said, 'From going to and fro on the earth, and from walking back and forth on it.' Then the LORD said to Satan, 'Have you considered My servant Job, that there is none like him on the earth, a blameless and upright man, one who fears God and shuns evil? And still he holds fast to his*

integrity, although you incited Me against him, to destroy him without cause.' So Satan answered the LORD and said, 'Skin for skin! Yes, all that a man has he will give for his life. But stretch out Your hand now, and touch his bone and his flesh, and he will surely curse You to Your face!' And the LORD said to Satan, 'Behold, he is in your hand, but spare his life.' So Satan went out from the presence of the LORD, and struck Job with painful boils from the sole of his foot to the crown of his head. And he took for himself a potsherd with which to scrape himself while he sat in the midst of the ashes. Then his wife said to him, 'Do you still hold fast to your integrity? Curse God and die!' But he said to her, 'You speak as one of the foolish women speaks. Shall we indeed accept good from God, and shall we not accept adversity?' In all this Job did not sin with his lips" (Job 2:1-10).

Here is the reason I wrote this book:

This statement that Job's wife uttered is well-known throughout Church history. It is the only statement of hers recorded in Scripture: *"Then his wife said to him, 'Do you still hold fast to your integrity? Curse God and die'"* (Job 2:9).

Over many years, for centuries, sermons have been preached about the terrible woman who, in her husband's lowest and darkest hour crushed him even further, saying, "Why don't you just curse God and die?" But remember: this is a respectable woman, a loving wife and mother, and one of the reasons Job had such favour with God.

Scripture tells us, *"The man who finds a wife finds a treasure, and he receives favor from the LORD"* (Proverbs 18:22, NLT). What I had failed to see was that she walked all the way through the suffering, pain, loss, and destruction *with* her husband. She was right there, probably next to him, when the messenger brought news that their children had been killed in a tornado and their livelihood was destroyed in a moment of time, and now she was dealing with the only thing left in her life—her husband! And he was covered head to toe with boils! How do you think she felt seeing him like that? Women are deeply connected emotionally with those around them, especially their family members. How much grief, sorrow, suffering, and pain could a woman take? Her emotions would have had to be shut down from what she witnessed during that short period of time when the various messengers brought their news.

In the ministry I have seen great pain and tragedy hit my own life as well as the lives of many of my church members. For example, I am reminded of a woman married to a man struggling with drug addiction. She stood by him for years. She had twin sons, and one of the sons died in the womb before she delivered them. I went to the hospital to support this couple, and met the woman in the emergency room. She asked me if I wanted to hold her child. The baby was wrapped in a blue blanket and was so tiny! I put him on my lap and pulled the blanket from his face. It was the dead son! I froze! I was speechless! I didn't know what to say or do. I felt so hopeless and defeated. The mom quietly told me the doctor had said that for her to hold the child would help heal her loss.

I fell apart and wept with that mother that day. She gathered strength through faith, got back up, and by God's grace is serving the Lord to this day, more than thirty years later. She is a heroine to me, an overcomer and a true champion of faith.

Another time, a dreadful tragedy struck on a Tuesday night while I was in a board meeting at WCF with my team. The custodian came to the door (this is before I had a cell phone). He said there was an emergency I had to attend to in Belle River, Ontario. A church member had been trimming his dad's trees when a branch fell on a hydro wire below, and electrocuted him. He died immediately, but they couldn't get his body down from the tree. Hydro had to shut down the power in the small town first. Meanwhile, the voltage kept charging through the man's body, burning it to a crisp. I got to the hospital just before the family came and was inside the waiting room when his mother and father came in. Their grieving was like nothing I've ever encountered. The pain in their cries and on their faces was beyond any grief I had ever seen. I didn't know what to do but to pray and stand alongside the man's loved ones. This was truly one of the most painful nights of my life, and my heart went out to this dear family.

One day, a newly-wed spouse came to the church office before the receptionist had arrived and was sitting in the lobby waiting for Cathy and me to come in. As I entered, I was taken aback to see this beautiful young woman looking like she had been in a car wreck. "He beat me up," she said. I was shocked, and felt her pain as her whole life was shattered and broken in a moment of time, due to abuse.

I can mention hundreds of tragedies I have personally witnessed and heard the stories, but they all lead me back to our heroine—Job's wife.

The Good News of the Bible is clear: for every "mistake and mess" we made, or in which we have been trapped, a "future message" follows. With God, even the most messed up ones can become masterpieces when it's all over. The bigger the mess, the bigger the miracle. And so it was for Job and his wife.

If you are going through a painful and disastrous time, don't give up, don't quit; things will turn around for you. Let the Good News shine a ray of hope into your broken heart. The best is yet to come for you in your life too, my friend, but only with God and through God.

CHAPTER TWO

Behind the Scenes of Spiritual Warfare

In Chapter One we made some important observations. Job and his wife were doing very well. They were rich, prosperous, and had been blessed with ten children and a very successful business. Then, tragedy struck the couple and, in a moment of time, they lost everything. Their world came crashing down.

We noted that the only conversation between Job and his wife recorded in Scripture is the following:

> *"So Satan went out from the presence of the LORD, and struck Job with painful boils from the sole of his foot to the crown of his head. And he took for himself a potsherd with which to scrape himself while he sat in the midst of the ashes. Then his wife said to him, "Do you still hold fast to your integrity? Curse God and die!" But he said to her, "You speak as one of the foolish women speaks. Shall we indeed accept good from God, and shall we not accept adversity?" In all this Job did not sin with his lips"* (Job 2:7-10).

These verses are packed with words containing revelation that gives us an understanding about the Accuser of the Brethren, who is none other than Satan, our adversary, our opponent:

> The one who comes to steal, kill and destroy.
> The one who desires to malign the character of God.
> The one who wants to distort and twist Scripture, to bring condemnation, guilt, shame, rejection, and inferiority against the people of God.

I have come to recognize that this Enemy is engaged in a violent spiritual battle against the Body of Christ, to knock good men and woman out of the race of faith, ruin their testimonies and marriages, slander their characters, malign their ministries, and steal their passion for God. Many are not even aware of the raging battle. Their ignorance and lack of knowledge give the Enemy the upper hand, to succeed in his attacks designed to knock them out of the fight and disqualify them from the race altogether. The Apostle Peter recognized this problem firsthand when Jesus told him that he was a target for Satan: *"Simon, Simon! Indeed, Satan has asked for you, that he may sift you as wheat. But I have prayed for you, that your faith should not fail; and when you have returned to Me, strengthen your brethren"* (Luke 22:31-32).

The word *sift* means "to test or examine carefully; to separate what is useful from what is not."

Just a few weeks ago, I needed a medical procedure, and my doctor set up an appointment at the hospital. I had to have a probe inserted in an uncomfortable area of my body. The probe was a tiny camera with a light to check what was going on inside my body. Fortunately, he found nothing out of the ordinary.

The way Satan sifted Peter reminded me of the probe. Satan was probing inside of him to see if the bold statements he was making were genuine—to see whether he really believed them. Peter shared about the trials and tests he experienced, in his Epistles, to encourage you and me the way Jesus encouraged him when he was being tested:

> *"Blessed be the God and Father of our LORD Jesus Christ, who according to His abundant mercy has begotten us again to a living hope through the resurrection of Jesus Christ from the dead, to an inheritance incorruptible and undefiled and that does not fade away, reserved in heaven for you, who are kept by the power of God through faith for salvation ready to be revealed in the last time. In this you greatly rejoice, though now for a little while, if need be, you have been grieved by various trials, that the genuineness of your faith, being much more precious than gold that perishes, though it is tested by fire, may be found to praise, honor, and glory at the revelation of Jesus Christ, whom having not seen you love. Though now you do not see Him, yet believing, you rejoice with joy inexpressible and full of glory, receiving the end of your faith—the salvation of your souls"* (1 Peter 1:3-9).

Notice how the great Apostle Peter shared about various trials of life. I am confident he was making reference to the conversation recorded in Luke 22 that he and Jesus had about Satan desiring to sift him as wheat to examine and test what was inside him.

Also, notice how he emphasized twice the genuineness of one's faith, and the reward of receiving as the outcome, salvation, deliverance, and freedom for the soul.

These blessings hark back to the sifting that Satan carried out with Peter: *"Beloved, do not think it strange concerning the fiery trial which is to try you, as though some strange thing happened to you; but rejoice to the extent that you partake of Christ's sufferings, that when His glory is revealed, you may also be glad with exceeding joy"* (1 Peter 4:12-13).

Peter is saying, don't be surprised at the fiery trials or calamities that come your way, but rejoice! I am confident he is speaking about the trial he endured during his denial of Christ. Three times he was knocked down, but not out of the race of faith, since he got back up again, and again, and again. He became a champion because he didn't quit.

Did he want to quit? Probably! He even said once, "I'm going back to fishing," but he didn't nurse that thought. He didn't stay or park on it. He went on to be a great man of God.

> *"Be sober, be vigilant; because your adversary the devil walks about like a roaring lion, seeking whom he may devour. Resist him, steadfast in the faith, knowing that the same sufferings are experienced by your brotherhood in the world. But may the God of all grace, who called us to His eternal glory by Christ Jesus, after you have suffered a while, perfect, establish, strengthen, and settle you. To Him be the glory and the dominion forever and ever. Amen"* (1 Peter 5:8-11).

That was Peter's firsthand experience with the Accuser, Tempter and Deceiver and, in the closing remarks of his first Epistle, he addressed clearly who the real Enemy was, and is, and how to oppose and resist him. He shared the importance of being *sober-minded*, meaning "marked by seriousness and habitual self-control."

Another word Peter uses is *vigilant*. It means to "keep awake and be watchful, to detect danger"—the Enemy's attacks that are being launched against your mind through lies, condemnation, shame, failure, fear, and intimidation. The Enemy is always looking for an open door into your life. He wants to devour your marriage, family, home, finances, health, and life, and always remember, his threefold purpose is to steal, kill, and destroy. Let's look at those words.

Steal means "to take away by unjust or unfair means, to get without earning, to accomplish in a concealed or unobserved manner, to steal small sums or petty objects, little by little." This is how the Enemy of souls operates, little by little, day by day—slowly and strategically he steals from our lives our peace, purpose, joy, and gratitude.

Klepto: this word refers to "one who steals secretly and effects his ends by force or intimidation." It means "to take the property of another wrongfully, and, especially, as a habitual or regular practice; to come or go secretly, unobtrusively, gradually, or unexpectedly."

I have recognized over many years of serving Christ, that God is just and fair, and the Enemy is unjust and unfair. He doesn't play fair, but stays hidden, works oftentimes unnoticed and secretly, and launches surprise attacks unexpectedly. The Enemy has convinced many Christians that he doesn't even exist, that it's just symbolic language, and so he goes unchecked and unnoticed; and so, we fight against one another not realizing who is behind it all.

Another strategy the Enemy of our souls launches against us is to kill.

Kill, or *immolate*, means "to rush, to slaughter for any purpose, to deprive of life, to deprive of activity or quality."

It's amazing, today, how many believers actually believe God is their problem. They think God is causing them pain and suffering, while the Enemy runs rampant in their lives. Instead of resisting, opposing, and fighting the Enemy, they cave in and believe it's part of God's will.

One of the greatest deceptions of the Enemy today is terminology. People will say, "Well, you know, God permitted it." That means God allowed it. I believe strongly that God has given you and me the authority over the Enemy. Jesus said.

"And I will give you the keys of the kingdom of heaven, and whatever you bind on earth will be bound in heaven, and whatever you loose on earth will be loosed in heaven" (Matthew 16:19).

We possess the keys of the Kingdom, and have authority over the works of darkness. It is our responsibility to arm ourselves with the full armor of God (Ephesians 6:10-16), and to resist the Devil. When we do, Scripture says, he will flee from us: *"Therefore submit to God. Resist the devil and he will flee from you"* (James 4:7).

It is our responsibility to learn the strategies of the evil one and not give him any place in our lives. We are to fight the good fight of faith, because God paid for it in full, and provided us with every weapon, strategy, and key to overcome the plots of the Enemy. After all, the Greater One lives inside us. The Warrior lives inside us. We need to know Christ as the Great Shepherd of the Church, but we also need to know Him as the Mighty God, the Champion, and the Warrior. We need to tap into the aggressive side of Christianity and kick the Devil's butt. God gave us authority to exercise and use daily against the Enemy, but if you don't believe this simple truth, then our Enemy has seeded a deceptive lie into your understanding. Never forget:

God is good,
God is just, and
God is faithful.

Destroy: "to ruin, devastate, render ineffective, nullify, defeat completely."

The final strategy of the Enemy is to destroy. *Destroy* means "to pull or tear down, to ruin completely beyond possibility of use, to paralyze completely."

The Devil wants to immobilize you, cripple you, bind you up, and shut you up. He would rather have you in Heaven, than on earth wreaking havoc on his Kingdom of darkness and overcoming him. Don't let him ruin your life! Rise up today as a champion in the army of the Lord. Rise up and decree with boldness the Word of God. *"If God is for us, who can be against us?"* (Romans 8:31). In all these circumstances we are more than conquerors (Romans 8:37).

Speak God's Word with authority, put on the entire armor of God, and battle the evil one. Tear down the mindsets and strongholds of unbelief and double-mindedness and stand against the Enemy:

> *"Finally, my brethren, be strong in the LORD and in the power of His might. Put on the whole armor of God, that you may be able to stand against the wiles of the devil. For we do not wrestle against flesh and blood, but against principalities, against powers, against the rulers of the darkness of this age, against spiritual hosts of wickedness in the heavenly places. Therefore take up the whole armor of God, that you may be able to withstand"* (Ephesians 6:10-13).

Notice, the Apostle Paul says five times *against, against, against, against, against*, which means "in resistance to or defense from."

Remember, Jesus knew Peter would repent after his fiery trial and encourage the brethren—the believers of Peter's day, and you and I today. Interesting that Jesus didn't pray for the Tempter to go away, but he prayed for Peter's faith not to fail. Why? Because faith is not a concept, experience, or movement. Our faith is in the person of Christ. Our trust, confidence, and assurance is that He is who He said He is, and He said what He meant.

Faith gets our prayers answered. We resist the Enemy by faith. Faith is a weapon. Scripture says, *"...taking the shield of faith"* (Ephesians 6:16).

We overcome the world by faith,
We receive forgiveness of sin by faith,
We are made righteous by faith,
We have freedom from spiritual death by faith,
We purify our hearts by faith,

We have access to the throne of grace by faith,
We have peace with God through faith,
We are adopted as His children through faith,
We have an inheritance by faith,
We understand that Satan hates our faith in God.

Satan gets stirred up when we speak words boldly in faith, share vision, and operate in the supernatural. He absolutely detests faith. This is the Apostle Peter's encouragement to those going through a storm, a challenge, or a tough time:

"So humble yourselves under the mighty power of God, and at the right time he will lift you up in honor. Give all your worries and cares to God, for he cares about you. Stay alert! Watch out for your great enemy, the devil. He prowls around like a roaring lion, looking for someone to devour. Stand firm against him, and be strong in your faith. Remember that your family of believers [Christian brothers and sisters] all over the world is [are] going through the same kind of suffering you are. In his kindness God called you to share in his eternal glory by means of Christ Jesus. So, after you have suffered a little while, he will restore, support, and strengthen you, and he will place you on a firm foundation. All power to him forever! Amen" (1 Peter 5:6-11, NLT).

How do we combat the Enemy? *"...above all, taking the shield of faith with which you will be able to quench all the fiery darts of the wicked one"* (Ephesians 6:16).

The Devil hurls slander and false accusations against our minds, over and over again, to wear us down and get a foothold in our minds.

Every one of us is a victim of these hits, fiery darts, and blows at one time or another. The hardest hits against my life have been missiles of betrayal that are a violation of trust. People I trusted turned against me, slandered, misrepresented, or lied about me, and twisted and distorted facts to cause hurt and pain. Has that happened to you? For me, the effects of a betrayal from more than thirty years ago are still there, although without the sting and associated pain.

For many years, I've made myself available in ministry to men who worked two jobs to make ends meet and put bread on the table, only to come home early one day due to sickness and find their wives in bed with another man. The same has happened to women.

I have heard stories of violations, injustices, abuse, revenge, and gossip, and have seen firsthand what bitterness can do to our hearts in relationships and homes.

I have seen good Christian men and woman take hits in life from the Enemy of our souls, and turn from a walk with God to soured, cold, hardened hearts. I have heard time after time, "So-and-so was a good man, or a good woman. Why did evil, or tragedy have to hit them in such a way?"

I have seen Christians make bad choices, suffer the consequences, and sadly, get mad or bitter at God. How unfair is that to our Lord?

Back to our text in Job:

> *"So Satan went out from the presence of the LORD, and struck Job with painful boils from the sole of his foot to the crown of his head. And he took for himself a potsherd with which to scrape himself while he sat in the midst of the ashes. Then his wife said to him, 'Do you still hold fast to your integrity? Curse God and die!' But he said to her, 'You speak as one of the foolish women speaks. Shall we indeed accept good from God, and shall we not accept adversity?' In all this Job did not sin with his lips"* (Job 2:7-10).

Job served God with the knowledge he had; he remained loyal and faithful to Him, but tragedy hit.

My friends, we live in a fallen world. Satan is the god of this world, according to Scripture, and he is in control of the hearts and minds of those who have not surrendered to the Lordship of Jesus, but are following their own selfish ways. Yet Job, whom God called a righteous man, was covered with boils from the top of his head to the bottom of his feet.

Boils usually start with a small, infected lump the size of a pea that is red and extremely painful when pus forms on top. This is followed by swelling, and it spreads rapidly over the body; then, fever hits, lymph nodes enlarge, and boils cover the entire body—not just the neck or buttocks, but the entire body; this had to be brutal for Job.

Not only had Job lost his ten children, servants, and livelihood, but now his health was severely compromised. He took a broken piece of pottery, sat in ashes, and scraped himself to alleviate the pain and the pus build-up. Quite certainly, bleeding occurred. This was a horrific and very serious condition, and extremely painful, with no reprieve. I have had one boil and it was painful and infected, but Job was covered in them.

Picture the poor guy sitting in ashes of repentance for this affliction. He didn't know why he had it, nor where it came from, but he said, *"'Shall we indeed accept good from God, and shall we not accept adversity?'* In all this Job did not sin with his lips" (Job 2:10).

Sadly, he believed God was afflicting him and causing the pain, trouble, and *adversity* (which means affliction, bad, calamity, grief, harm, hurt, ill, mischief, misery, sorrow, wickedness, and trouble) he was experiencing. He didn't have the understanding we have today of spiritual warfare. Neither did he have knowledge of the evil one. He was in the dark concerning these spiritual things when he spoke these words:

> "Then the LORD answered Job out of the whirlwind, and said: 'Who is this who darkens counsel by words without knowledge? Now prepare yourself like a man; I will question you, and you shall answer Me. Where were you when I laid the foundations of the earth? Tell Me, if you have understanding. Who determined its measurements? Surely you know! Or who stretched the line upon it? To what were its foundations fastened? Or who laid its cornerstone, when the morning stars sang together, and all the sons of God shouted for joy?'" (Job 38:1-7).

First, God asked Job question after question, and then He said: "Shall the one who contends with the Almighty correct Him? He who rebukes God, let him answer it" (Job 40:1-2).

Job answered: "Behold, I am vile; what shall I answer You? I lay my hand over my mouth. Once I have spoken, but I will not answer; yes, twice, but I will proceed no further" (Job 40:3-4).

God challenged Job. He "answered Job out of the whirlwind, and said: 'Now prepare yourself like a man; I will question you, and you shall answer Me'" (Job 40:6-7).

Then, Job responded: "You asked, 'Who is this who hides counsel without knowledge?' Therefore I have uttered what I did not understand, things too wonderful for me, which I did not know" (Job 42:3).

Wow! Wow! Wow! How powerful is this discourse with facts from God Himself!

But now, let's return to the story of Job's wife and her response.

> "Then his wife said to him, 'Do you still hold fast to your integrity? Curse God and die!' But he said to her, 'You speak as one of the foolish women speaks. Shall we indeed

accept good from God, and shall we not accept adversity?' In all this Job did not sin with his lips" (Job 2:9-10).

In the next chapter we will look at the response Job's wife gave. Questions to ask ourselves may be as follows:

- Have we been blaming God for our problems?
- Are we mad, or angry at God? If yes, then, why?
- Have we been resisting and withstanding the Enemy's plans and lies, or entertaining them in our minds?
- Do we really believe that God is Good?
- Do we understand that we are in a spiritual battle?
- Do we believe that Satan is a real person with a real personality?
- Do we understand that in the Bible, things are truly stated at times, but not necessarily statements of God's truth?

CHAPTER THREE

The Pain in the Storm

"So Satan went out from the presence of the LORD, and struck Job with painful boils from the sole of his foot to the crown of his head. And he took for himself a potsherd with which to scrape himself while he sat in the midst of the ashes. Then his wife said to him, 'Do you still hold fast to your integrity? Curse God and die!' But he said to her, 'You speak as one of the foolish women speaks. Shall we indeed accept good from God, and shall we not accept adversity?' In all this Job did not sin with his lips" (Job 2:7-10).

Who was Job's wife? We don't know her name. We don't know her background. We don't know anything about her family heritage, or who her Dad or Mom were. We don't know in which town she was born, or where she lived when growing up. All we know is that she was married to Job, had ten children, and made a statement that was forever recorded in biblical history.

As we consider this statement, let's remember that this was the same woman who had seen, with her own eyes, the messengers who brought bad news about her children. What kind of impact would that have had on her?

Over the years, I have witnessed many good mothers who have had miscarriages. The grief in their hearts from the loss of life of their children was devastating for them. It took them many years to work through their pain.

Abortion can leave even greater scars. I have met precious women who have had abortions and, after coming to Christ, they have recognized the magnitude of what happened during the termination of the life of the child they once carried. Their guilt and pain, compounded by resulting depression and sorrow, have often been inconsolable even many years later. The good news is that those children are in Heaven, and that their mothers will see them again. King David, who also lost a child, said, *"I shall go to him, but he shall not return to me."*

> *"And he said, 'While the child was alive, I fasted and wept; for I said, "Who can tell whether the LORD will be gracious to me, that the child may live?" But now he is dead; why should I fast? Can I bring him back again? I shall go to him, but he shall not return to me'"* (2 Samuel 12:22-23).

Cathy and I had neighbors next door, who we got to know very well when we first were married and lived in our first house. Then, one night, the oldest daughter, who was sixteen, was out with friends and was killed in a car wreck. After that day, seeing her father and mother was never the same. There was deep sorrow in their hearts at the loss of their oldest daughter. The pain and sorrow continued for many years, and every year the parents visited the site of the accident, brought flowers, and wept. The loss of their precious daughter was heart-wrenching and incredibly painful.

When only grief is left, it can itself be the memory. To this day, many years later, my mother-in-law still feels pain at the passing of her daughter Jennifer. Still every year she goes to the cemetery, brings flowers, and prays. Death is never easy. It is called an enemy in Scripture—the last enemy to be destroyed—because of the pain, sorrow and sadness it inflicts. *"The last enemy that will be destroyed is death"* (1 Corinthians 15:26).

There was Momma, next to her beloved husband when this news arrived. Read these verses again very carefully and thoughtfully. Put yourself in this woman's place for that one moment when she heard the reports of disaster, calamity and death.

> *"Now there was a day when his sons and daughters were eating and drinking wine in their oldest brother's house; and a messenger came to Job and said, 'The oxen were plowing and the donkeys feeding beside them, when the Sabeans raided them and took them away—indeed they have killed the servants with the edge of the sword; and I alone have escaped to tell you!' While he was still speaking, another also came and said, 'The fire of God fell from heaven and burned up the sheep and the servants, and consumed them; and I alone have escaped to tell you!' While he was still speaking, another also came and said, 'The Chaldeans formed three bands, raided the camels and took them away, yes, and killed the servants with the edge of the sword; and I alone have*

escaped to tell you!' While he was still speaking, another also came and said, 'Your sons and daughters were eating and drinking wine in their oldest brother's house, and suddenly a great wind came from across the wilderness and struck the four corners of the house, and it fell on the young people, and they are dead; and I alone have escaped to tell you!'" (Job 1:13-19).

Notice it says, "*Now there was a day....*" Have you ever sensed it was going to be "one of those days?" We say that because, usually, at the start of the day something upsetting happens, and then shortly afterwards, something else. I think, at times, all of us have said, after some challenges, "It's been a [fill in the blank] ____ kind of a da —a tough day, a challenging day," or as some say, "It's the story of my life!" But likely none of us have had a day like that one day was for Job's wife.

Look at what happened in just one day to her, and notice also the timing: as one bad report came in, another was on the way. "*While he was still speaking...*" is stated three times. As the old, worldly saying goes, "When it rains it pours."

I have had some very tough days in my life, but nothing compared to what Job and his wife experienced. Think about all these things happening to a couple in one day: the loss of a thousand oxen, five hundred female donkeys, and all the workers who took care of them. At least fifty servants were killed when the Sabeans came and stole the animals. Imagine the financial devastation that took place, and the grief of telling the families—spouses, children, uncles, and aunts of their employees, that their husbands or wives had just been killed in a storm.

It didn't stop there. While one was sharing, another arrived to say that all the sheep and servants were killed by a fire from Heaven. A brush fire? A meteor? There were seven thousand sheep corpses and probably a few hundred servants' bodies on the ground charred by fire. What a sight!

The after-effects of this loss would have been horrendous.

The loss of their employees would have had a profound impact on the couple, but worst, yet again, having to break the news to their families. Imagine having to sift through charred rubble to identify loved ones. Imagine how the survivor might have felt at the death of all of his coworkers. The devastation of the trauma had to be overwhelming.

This reminds me of the most painful day that Pastor Cathy went through when coming home from the Kitchener Market with a friend. The police were in the driveway with the bad news, "We believe your husband, Jim Doyle, was killed in a car wreck this morning. Could you come and identify the body at the morgue!" How deep was that pain? Then she had to tell her three beautiful daughters, "Your dad is not coming home again. He was killed in a car accident!" The grief and the despair had to be overwhelming for her and the girls.

Could things get worse for Job and his wife? While that one was speaking, another came to report that three bands of Chaldeans had raided, taken Job's three thousand camels, and killed all the servants. Only one had escaped.

More financial devastation. Perhaps another seventy-five to one hundred families to inform. Imagine going to their homes, and breaking the news. Imagine the grief, bitterness, anger, hurt, pain, and weeping.

Then came the final blow. While the messenger spoke, another came, saying a great wind—possibly a tornado—hit the house where their children were partying, and none survived. We don't know who else was in that house that day—grandkids; great-grandkids; relatives; neighbours; family friends; aunts or uncles. Now, all were dead. How does a couple recover? Again, imagine the horror this couple felt—the weeping, screaming, and pain.

Just so you know, the story didn't end here. Restoration beyond what they could imagine, was yet to come. I am setting up the scenario of the real-life tragedy that preceded the victory.

We have all experienced challenging times, painful situations, and embarrassing ones, but not like those Jesus experienced on the Cross. He was even, prophetically, called a Man of Sorrows: *"He is despised and rejected by men, a Man of sorrows and acquainted with grief. And we hid, as it were, our faces from Him; He was despised, and we did not esteem Him"* (Isaiah 53:3).

This Scripture describes the trial the Son of God endured on our behalf at Calvary. Notice the words despised, rejected, Man of Sorrows, grief; they all speak to the root of his overwhelming emotional pain and anxiety.

In my opinion, Job and his wife take second place to Jesus with all the traumatization they experienced in this season of their lives.

More than thirty-one years ago, when Cathy and I were married at Toronto's Evangel Temple, we had a beautiful wedding. Her church in Mississauga and WCF joined together to celebrate. But on our first Sunday back from our honeymoon, we discovered we had lost about a quarter of our congregation in a church split. The timing was the worst, the pain was deep, and the trauma drained me of enthusiasm and energy for a long time. Every time another family left, the grief and sorrow I experienced for myself, and on their behalf, was torturous—very difficult for a Pastor to see, and debilitating because of the helplessness to prevent it. Along with others, I had to hear and endure negative, demoralizing statements spoken to my face that ripped me apart inside. But God restored and turned things around, and almost half of those who left came back over the years.

Trauma can come in many ways and forms and is never easy to endure. How many people have we met over the years who were traumatized and their lives seem to stop in the tracks of that experience, event, or painful memory. Over the years, in ministry, I have seen and heard the stories of folks traumatized by a cruel parent, stepparent, relative, or friend. One incredible friend, shared about the abusiveness of his dad toward him, and his brothers and sisters, and how he struggled with forgiveness toward his father.

Most of us reading this, have had traumatic experiences hit our life at one time or another. In the movie *Hope Floats* there was a scene where a couple was fighting, and the husband told his wife he wanted a divorce because he was leaving her for another woman. The young daughter overheard the conversation, and went and packed her suitcase because she was going off with her daddy. He tells her she can't come with him, and the child screams how she wants to be with her daddy, and runs after his car down the street. The trauma of rejection and abandonment that little girl experienced can affect her for many years in her life.

On Encounter Weekends, over many years, with men on a two-day experience to connect with God and deal with issues affecting our lives, so many share what is commonly known as the "Father Wound." The "Father Wound" is a hurt, rejection, abandonment, or abuse that came from their dads. Our team has recognized that almost half the men coming on the weekends are carrying a deep "Father Wound." Many men were put down, shamed, humiliated, and called names of every kind, usually not in a positive way. The hurt and unforgiveness is often the root issue they are carrying into their relationships.

I remember, many years ago, my wife Cathy said, after a phone conversation I was having with an individual that caused me much pain and wounded me deeply, "You haven't forgiven her." My defenses immediately went up and I said I had forgiven her. Now I was mad at Cathy for telling me that. I learned an incredible lesson that day that, there are two kinds of forgiveness—one is from our heads, and the other is from our hearts. I mentally assented forgiveness from my head, and actually believed I had forgiven her, but she could still push my buttons and get me upset.

I believe many Christians are where I was at; they forgive, but it's not from their hearts—it's from their minds. That day it shifted from my head to my heart, and I immediately experienced a release inside, and genuine forgiveness was given from my heart that day.

I'm sensing as you're reading this story, it's resonated inside you. Just stop and simply ask the Holy Spirit to help you shift Christ's forgiveness from your head to your heart, and mean it; and watch what happens—"freedom inside."

Oftentimes, people become extremely moody and can isolate themselves from friends and family. These would be the folks that have a hard time relaxing. They may always seem uptight and reactive. They may also have a hard time concentrating, and, oftentimes, have great difficulty learning life's lessons. They can have ongoing bad dreams and even frightful nightmares.

The root of these behaviors and other problems is often trauma and mental assent forgiveness. Get to the root, and you can deal with the fruit! Pray inner healing to undo the damage caused by the traumatic experiences, and in Jesus' Name cast out the spirit of fear from your life.

Some traumatized folks struggle with extreme depression, obsessions, and even suicidal thoughts. I'm convinced that many adults who have never dealt with trauma from their childhoods, or their past, disconnect and become relationally challenged. The problems from their past surface, and they struggle with current conflicts, because the current ones trigger past memories and cause them to react. I'm convinced the doorway into substance abuse is widened where past trauma, violations, and abuse are present and never dealt with, but stuffed emotionally down inside us.

The trauma I suffered as a young child, caused me to become very angry, fighting, and having fits of rage at times. I have learned the hard way that, in life, attitudes are important for success and for God's blessings being released upon our lives.

I sense this chapter is triggering some deep emotions in some readers. Please don't stop reading. You don't have to live the victim mentality any longer. The answer is in the next few chapters.

God sees you as a champion. You don't have to park in the trauma. Rather, forgive, by the grace of God, those who harmed you and make a choice to get up and

live again,
breathe again,
flourish again,
enjoy life once again.

God is for you. He is on your side and He is the God who Restores. Let's pray:

Heavenly Father, heal my heart, mind, emotions, and body of every event in my life that has been traumatic and has paralyzed me. Help me to forgive and release the ones who caused the trauma to my life, in Jesus' Name.

Help me to get out of the ruts in life and start moving forward once again, in Jesus' Name.

I let go of all hurts, lies, abuse, shame, and wounds that have been spoken and carried out against my life. I release them, and choose to release and resist the strongholds in my mind from this day forward, in Jesus' Name.

"The LORD is my shepherd; I shall not want. He makes me to lie down in green pastures; He leads me beside the still waters. He restores my soul" (Psalm 23:1-3).

"He restores my soul;" the literal translation is, "He is re-establishing my life." My friend, God is getting your life back for you. It's not your circumstances; it's not your spouse; it's not your finances; it's God who causes your life to return. Somebody reading this is getting it! It's God who restores your life. Don't wait till the next chapter, but speak this out now:

The Pain in the Storm

My God is restoring my soul!
My God is causing my life to be re-established!
My God is giving me new life, abundant life, peaceful life.
My God is giving me back the enjoyment I once had!
My God is the One who restores!
My God is replenishing my life, filling me with hope, filling me with strength, filling me with joy unspeakable!
My God is a restoring God!
My life will not be characterized by the damage of the past!
My God in the present is with me.
He will help me, He will encourage me!
He is restoring my soul, my mind, and my damaged emotions!

He is the God of Restoration. The word *restore* means "to re-establish by bringing back into existence."

> *"The LORD will guide you continually, giving you water when you are dry and restoring your strength. You will be like a well-watered garden, like an ever-flowing spring. Some of you will rebuild the deserted ruins of your cities. Then you will be known as a rebuilder of walls and a restorer of homes"* (Isaiah 58:11-12, NLT).

I have seen the restoration of the Lord in my personal life many times, and I am so grateful for His mercy and goodness. This is why I want to share with you about the God who restores.

By this time, I trust that your hope is rising, your faith is being strengthened, and your future is becoming clearer. Let's look at how God restores and causes our lives to return again.

Job's wife was traumatized greatly. She was devastated emotionally, overwhelmed with grief, and grieving her losses. Now her husband, her pillar of strength, lover, and father to their children was in his lowest moment of life—devastated, fearful, worried, suffering—and she, through damaged emotions, said to him, *"Do you still hold fast to your integrity? Curse God and die"* (Job 2:9)!

Now we understand a bit of why she said it, but there is great news ahead for her and her husband, as the God who Restores comes on the scene.

Are you feeling overwhelmed by life's blows? Or perhaps you are greatly discouraged from sustaining hit after hit, blow after blow? Maybe you are confused and troubled and are questioning God. But never forget: Jesus tells you today, my friend, *"The thief does not come except to steal, and to kill, and to destroy. I have come that they may have life, and that they may have it more abundantly"* (John 10:10).

Believe Rick 101! God is not your problem! The Enemy is! He is real, so start resisting him today.

The time period for the Book of Job was approximately nine months. Nine is a significant number spiritually in the Bible:

- Normal pregnancy is nine months to delivery or completion.
- There are nine gifts of the Spirit and nine fruits of the Spirit.
- In the ninth hour on the cross, Jesus gave up His spirit.
- Jesus appeared to His disciples nine times after His resurrection.
- An angel of the Lord visited Cornelius at the ninth hour of the day.
- The testing of Job and his wife lasted nine months.

Why are we looking at these points? They will help us understand the verses immediately following the tragedies Job and his wife shared. We saw how the deaths, loss, destruction, and pain culminated in the worst day of this couple's life. Shortly after, as Job's wife was suffering alongside her husband in his illness, she commented to him, *"Do you still hold fast to your integrity? Curse God and die!"* But he reprimanded her: *"'You speak as one of the foolish women speaks. Shall we indeed accept good from God, and shall we not accept adversity?'"* (Job 2:9-10). Job did not sin with his words.

Let's look more in depth at Job's wife's statement.

The first thing to note is that she spoke out of the bitterness of her heart. Both she and Job believed that God was somehow responsible for their suffering and that he had afflicted them. Thus Job said, *"Shall we indeed accept good from God and shall we not accept adversity?"* Again I emphasize: they did not have the knowledge we have today of the spiritual realm, of the Accuser of the Brethren—the one who twists the facts, and twists and distorts the true character of God. With both of them at their lowest point, the wife said, *"Do you still hold fast to your integrity?"*

Integrity is defined as "wholeness, entireness, completeness; a state of being unified." Its root word means intact, untouched, and entire." In simple language, integrity means our words and deeds line up. They are unified. *Integrity* also speaks of "credibility, trust, and confidence in the followers." People of integrity have nothing to hide and nothing to fear. Their lives are transparent.

We see in the Book of Job, however, that in his lowest moment of life his helpmeet questioned his integrity—the lowest shot she could have taken. She even followed it up with, *"Curse God and die!"* In other words, God did this, so speak evil to your God!

The word *curse* is an expression of a wish that misfortune, evil, or doom would befall someone, in this case, God. Not only that, but, "Just end your misery, my husband and die!" Those were probably the most hurtful words she had spoken to her husband in their entire marriage. Job reacted, saying, "You speak as one of the foolish women speaks."

Now the two of them were in a war of words. Has anybody been there? You say something bad or mean to me, and I will give you back your own medicine. A war of words!

Job called his wife *foolish*, meaning she was a stupid, wicked, vile, wretched, highly offensive, unpleasant, repulsive, disgusting, depraved, despicable person. How brutal is that! Do you think they might perhaps have been happy with one another at that time?

Remember, the purpose for our examination of these interactions in detail, is to demonstrate the effects of trauma on all our lives: the pain trauma causes so that we can't even think or speak right, and the reactions, in addition to the bitterness we might feel, because of the circumstances of life that have devastated us.

I identify with those feelings. I have said things when I was in great pain due to events in my life, and I am not proud of my words. I wish I had never uttered them, but they couldn't be retracted. What could I do? I could only go to God. I repented, and the hardest thing to do was to forgive myself for messing up.

This altercation between Job and his wife would have taken place during the first week or so, of the first of the nine months in total before their restoration.

How would it be possible for this couple ever to move forward, away from this grief?

How could they ever enjoy intimacy with one another as a couple again?

How could they ever forgive one another for the hurtful words they had shared?

We will answer these questions, but first, my questions to you are:

If you had been in the same situation, how would you have reacted?

If you had lost everything you possessed including your children and loved ones, how would you have reacted?

These are tough questions, yet for Job and his wife they were reality.

We all face tragedies of some sort in life. To admit it is not to speak a negative confession, but rather to acknowledge a fact. We all face troubled waters. We all face betrayals, rejection, shame, inferiority, and pain of some kind. Some of us experience more of these trials than others. Peter said, "Don't think it's strange! Such events are not weird. They are part of living in a fallen world where Satan is the god in control of the hearts and minds of those who have not yet yielded to the Lordship of Jesus Christ in their lives."

God gave mankind His Word to teach to our children so that generations after us might live right and follow the ways of the Lord—live blessed, prosperous, and fruitful lives that affect other generations to come.

When we act on the Word of God and resist the Enemy of our souls on every front, we enter into the abundant life. The abundant life doesn't "just happen" without our engagement—without a fight, battle, challenge, or opportunity. If we are to live the abundant life, trials will hit all of us at one time or another.

In the next chapter, I will focus on what we have to do to get back up again once we have been struck down with tragedy. How can we begin to breathe again and live as overcomers? How can we be like Job's wife, the secret heroine of the Bible?

Be like *Job's wife*? The *"heroine"*? I am sure you are wondering and waiting at this point to see how this author develops his premise. No jumping to the end of the book for a preview! Please enjoy the story as it unfolds.

CHAPTER FOUR

Digging Out of the Ashes

We have looked at the conflict between Job and his wife—their exchange of harsh words due to their anguish and bitterness of soul. It is amazing that throughout their ordeal, according to Scripture, Job said nothing wrong. He maintained his integrity before the Lord even in the most severe testing of the human soul and emotions.

God is bigger than our present pain and circumstances and has perfect understanding of the grief of the human heart and soul. He restores and forgives quickly.

Let's keep this Scripture before us:

"Then his wife said to him, 'Do you still hold fast to your integrity? Curse God and die!' But he said to her, 'You speak as one of the foolish women speaks. Shall we indeed accept good from God, and shall we not accept adversity?' In all this Job did not sin with his lips. Now when Job's three friends heard of all this adversity that

had come upon him, each one came from his own place— Eliphaz the Temanite, Bildad the Shuhite, and Zophar the Naamathite. For they had made an appointment together to come and mourn with him, and to comfort him. And when they raised their eyes from afar, and did not recognize him, they lifted their voices and wept; and each one tore his robe and sprinkled dust on his head toward heaven. So they sat down with him on the ground seven days and seven nights, and no one spoke a word to him, for they saw that his grief was very great" (Job 2:9-13).

I have noticed that when people are in grief and intense pain, some good-meaning folks come along to try to encourage them. So it was with Job. Notice that when his friends Eliphaz, Bildad, and Zophar saw Job from afar, they didn't even recognize him. They lifted their voices and wept. Each one tore his robe and sprinkled dust on his head toward Heaven. They were shocked at the severity of Job's condition. Their motive was to try to comfort their friend and encourage him, and incredibly, for seven days and nights, not one of them spoke a word to Job, and, probably, neither to his wife. She was likely there with him, although it is not recorded in Scripture.

These three men, possibly Rabbis, knew a fair amount about God and had strong theological opinions.

For our purposes, we don't need to analyze their dialogue with Job, but when seven days and nights had passed without conversation, *"...Job opened his mouth and cursed the day of his birth. And Job spoke, and said: 'May the day perish on which I was born, and the night in which it was said, "A male child is conceived"'"* (Job 3:1-3).

Job, feeling defeated and hopeless, cursed the day he was born, and the night in which he was conceived. Despair must have overwhelmed him and his wife.

After he bared his soul, his friends began to speak. First Eliphaz the Temanite: He accused Job of having sinned. He insisted it was all Job's fault, and that the chastening was from the Lord.

In the next two chapters it states that Job defended himself, and then Bildad the Shuhite answered, saying Job should repent.

Job responded in chapters nine and ten. Then Zophar the Naamathite answered also saying, "Repent! It's your fault!"

It's not surprising that when we are engaged in a spiritual battle, we need people to intercede alongside us and stand in prayer with us. Too many want to point the finger in blame and bury the one who is in the struggle.

I won't develop the entire discourse, but clearly it upset God. We see God's comments in the last chapter of Job. They will now be the focus of our study.

"Then Job answered the LORD and said: 'I know that You can do everything, and that no purpose of Yours can be withheld from You. You asked, "Who is this who hides counsel without knowledge?" Therefore I have uttered what I did not understand, things too wonderful for me, which I did not know. Listen, please, and let me speak; You said, "I will question you, and you shall answer Me." I have heard of You by the hearing of the ear, but now my eye sees You. Therefore I abhor myself, and repent in dust and ashes.'

"And so it was, after the LORD had spoken these words to Job, that the LORD said to Eliphaz the

Temanite, 'My wrath is aroused against you and your two friends, for you have not spoken of Me what is right, as My servant Job has. Now therefore, take for yourselves seven bulls and seven rams, go to My servant Job, and offer up for yourselves a burnt offering; and My servant Job shall pray for you. For I will accept him, lest I deal with you according to your folly; because you have not spoken of Me what is right, as My servant Job has.'

"So Eliphaz the Temanite and Bildad the Shuhite and Zophar the Naamathite went and did as the LORD commanded them; for the LORD had accepted Job. And the LORD restored Job's losses when he prayed for his friends. Indeed the LORD gave Job twice as much as he had before. Then all his brothers, all his sisters, and all those who had been his acquaintances before, came to him and ate food with him in his house; and they consoled him and comforted him for all the adversity that the LORD had brought upon him. Each one gave him a piece of silver and each a ring of gold.

"Now the LORD blessed the latter days of Job more than his beginning; for he had fourteen thousand sheep, six thousand camels, one thousand yoke of oxen, and one thousand female donkeys. He also had seven sons and three daughters. And he called the name of the first Jemimah, the name of the second Keziah, and the name of the third Keren-Happuch. In all the land were found no women so beautiful as the daughters of Job; and their father gave them an inheritance among their brothers. After this Job lived one hundred and forty years, and saw his children and grandchildren for four generations. So Job died, old and full of days" (Job 42).

The first thing we see is that Job repented for everything he had spoken against God: *"I take back everything I said, and I sit in dust and ashes to show my repentance"* (Job 42:6, NLT). Pretty strong words from Job, meaning, "I am sorry, broken, humbled by every word I said." No doubt he had spoken out of the bitterness of his heart, from the incredible excruciating pain he was suffering, and God surely forgave him.

This brings me to a very important point I've learned about God: He is not surprised when His children vent to Him. Let me say it plainly: God is a safe person with whom to vent, share our pain, anger, frustrations, troubling thoughts, and difficult times. God loves us and is committed to our well-being, even if we have sworn at Him, yelled at Him, or given Him a piece of our mind; He still loves us and believes in us.

God finished speaking to Job and turned to Job's friend Eliphaz.

> *"And so it was, after the LORD had spoken these words to Job, that the LORD said to Eliphaz the Temanite, 'My wrath is aroused against you and your two friends, for you have not spoken of Me what is right, as My servant Job has. Now therefore, take for yourselves seven bulls and seven rams, go to My servant Job, and offer up for yourselves a burnt offering; and My servant Job shall pray for you. For I will accept him, lest I deal with you according to your folly; because you have not spoken of Me what is right, as My servant Job has.' So Eliphaz the Temanite and Bildad the Shuhite and Zophar the Naamathite went and did as the LORD commanded them; for the LORD had accepted Job"* (Job 42:7-9).

How would you like God to say, "My wrath is aroused against you and your two friends." The word *wrath* means "the rapid breathing of passionate anger shown on one's countenance." Whatever that means, I wouldn't want God ticked off at me.

Job's friends repented, brought a sacrifice, and Job prayed for them. The Lord accepted their prayers and the friends went on with their lives.

In the next verse a shift takes place. Up to this point it has been about nine months from the beginning of Job's sorrows. The subsequent words are powerful, and very refreshing to Job and his wife. These verses are mind-blowing:

> *"And the LORD restored Job's losses when he prayed for his friends. Indeed the LORD gave Job twice as much as he had before. Then all his brothers, all his sisters, and all those who had been his acquaintances before, came to him and ate food with him in his house; and they consoled him and comforted him for all the adversity that the LORD had brought upon him. Each one gave him a piece of silver and each a ring of gold. Now the LORD blessed the latter days of Job more than his beginning; for he had fourteen thousand sheep, six thousand camels, one thousand yoke of oxen, and one thousand female donkeys. He also had seven sons and three daughters. And he called the name of the first Jemimah, the name of the second Keziah, and the name of the third Keren-Happuch. In all the land were found no women so beautiful as the daughters of Job; and their father gave them an inheritance among their brothers. After this Job lived one hundred and forty years, and saw his children*

and grandchildren for four generations. So Job died, old and full of days" (Job 42:10-17).

How powerful is prayer! When Job prayed for his three friends God restored double the blessing, anointing, and provision upon his life.

That is our God! Just as He did for Job, He does for us. Thirty-five years ago, a long-time friend of mine from Detroit, the late Dr. Charles O. Miles, prophesied over me, "Rick, God is going to give you double for all the trouble you been through." I really didn't understand that word at the time, but knew there was a principle in Scripture about Elisha receiving a double portion: *"Instead of your shame, you shall have double honor, and instead of confusion, they shall rejoice in their portion. Therefore in their land they shall possess double; everlasting joy shall be theirs"* (Isaiah 61:7).

I have seen the mercy, grace, and the hand of God upon my life from the day I received that word until today. The double blessing continues to come to pass. My church has doubled. My anointing has doubled. When I married Cathy years later, my children doubled from three to six. I got double the house. My brown-eyed girl Cathy is doubly gifted, anointed, and walks closely with God with the double-portion anointing. I am a blessed man by God's great grace and mercy.

Notice when this doubling of blessing happened to Job: it happened when Job prayed for his friends who had said unkind things against him. They had made some very strong accusations and had spoken condemnation over him.

I have learned to bless men and women who speak negatively, critically, and judgmentally against me and the ministry God entrusted to me. Over many decades, when fellow ministers from my community spoke evil, condemnation, or lies about me, belittling, or even mocking me or WCF, I chose not to retaliate, but blessed them.

A fellow Pastor in Windsor, tore my church down every week on his Saturday evening radio program. He listened to my sermons and constantly tried to find fault with me and the doctrine I preached.

When people criticize me, I examine my heart openly and honestly, and ask myself if there is any truth to what they are saying. If there is not, then I move on with life. If I am doing wrong, then I make the necessary adjustments in agreement with the teaching in Matthew 5:11-12: *"Blessed are you when they revile and persecute you, and say all kinds of evil against you falsely for My sake. Rejoice and be exceedingly glad, for great is your reward in heaven, for so they persecuted the prophets who were before you."*

According to these verses, if someone has spoken lies and evil against you falsely, then they have laid up a great big, mega-huge reward for you in Heaven. If you really believe that, then you can thank them and say, "Here is a monetary gift to let you know I appreciate you laying up a great big gift for me in Heaven!" This is a principle of life for Cathy and I that has worked for us many times over the years. We really believe it, and it's a powerful tool against unkind things and acts people do toward us.

I did this to critics for more than thirty years in Windsor, and I sent out thousands of dollars over the years to bless my enemies. The majority of them have turned away from their criticisms and become my friends in the community.

They say money can't buy you love, but it's not true. Money wasn't the motive for their change of heart, but it prepared the way for them to open up and learn about WCF and its love for our community, Canada, and Christ.

Maybe it's time right now for you to consider your relationships. Are some broken?

Maybe it's time to pray for your former friends, or present enemies—to let go of offence.

Maybe it's debt cancellation time for some deeply wounded areas of your soul that God wants to heal.

Maybe it's time to put the axe to the root of bitterness that has hindered and blocked your future, to allow the wounds of betrayal to be released, and begin to heal. Meditating on a life of regrets with its "could haves," "would haves," and "should haves" won't help you one bit, but praying sincerely for God's grace, mercy, and forgiveness will release you, also, and cause the restoration to take place. I am hearing God say very strongly:

Forgive now!
Cancel the debt now!
Your future depends on the decisions you make today.
Release the abuser now!
Release the betrayer now!
Release the shameful past now!
Release the self-hatred and destructive spirit now!
Release the fear and imprisonment of your mind now!
It's debt cancellation time toward others and yourself!
Breathe deeply.
It's a new day.
The lights are going back on.
The depression is lifting!
The obsession is broken!

Your sleep will be sweet and uninterrupted.
Your countenance will undergo a noticeable change.
Your relationships are going to flourish again.
Above all, your walk with God is going to a new level!
Stop and give God an offering of thanksgiving.

I'm also sensing strongly to quote Romans 12:19-21:

"Beloved, do not avenge yourselves, but rather give place to wrath; for it is written, 'Vengeance is Mine, I will repay,' says the LORD. Therefore 'If your enemy is hungry, feed him; if he is thirsty, give him a drink; for in so doing you will heap coals of fire on his head.' Do not be overcome by evil, but overcome evil with good."

Stop trying to take out vengeance on the betrayer.
Stop the vengeance toward the teenage son who betrayed you and stole money from you.
Stop the vengeance toward your former church leader.
Stop the vengeance toward that ex-spouse.
Do it now and cut the supply line
from hell off your life today.
Give God thanks.
Do it now.

Take ten minutes of your time and thank God for His peace, His forgiveness, His joy, His refreshing, His mercy, and now His restoration. They are yours. Your restoration will start today.

It's a new day, my friend!

God's a restoring God. After the test of life, the test of faith, the darkest hour, there is a breakthrough on the other side. Look what happened to Job:

Digging Out of the Ashes   73

> *"And the LORD restored Job's losses when he prayed for his friends. Indeed the LORD gave Job twice as much as he had before. Then all his brothers, all his sisters, and all those who had been his acquaintances before, came to him and ate food with him in his house; and they consoled him and comforted him for all the adversity that the LORD had brought upon him. Each one gave him a piece of silver and each a ring of gold. Now the LORD blessed the latter days of Job more than his beginning; for he had fourteen thousand sheep, six thousand camels, one thousand yoke of oxen, and one thousand female donkeys. He also had seven sons and three daughters"* (Job 42:10-13).

Job had double for all his trouble. Notice the Lord gave Job twice as much as he had before. He was the richest man in the land before. Now he was doubly rich because God chose to make him rich.

Interesting that during Job's suffering, many folks pulled away from him. Has that ever happened to you—when you were down friends didn't visit you, or may even have forgotten about you?

It reminds me of what happened to my childhood friend back in high school. One day he was doing his paper route and fell and broke a bone. When they x-rayed the broken bone, they found a cancerous tumor in his hip. It was by accident that they found it. He went through a tough time with bone cancer and treatments, and many of his friends pulled away. Later, the cancer went into remission and he married a lovely young woman. She was a blessing. I was best man at their wedding. They had a son, and then the cancer came back and took his life. Many friends came to the funeral, paid their respects, and apologized for pulling away.

Sometimes, when someone is going through a challenge it's easy to pull away, but in a faith community we need to pull together.

I was just with a friend recently and heard he was going through a few bumps in his journey of faith. I tracked him down. He was appreciative for that, but said his small group from church was looking after him constantly. How good is that? It's probably good for each of us to connect with a small group in church.

Similarly for Job and his wife, their family abandoned them, but came back. Job's brothers, sisters, and former acquaintances each brought gifts of silver or gold and comforted and encouraged him. Understand this benevolence wasn't just for Job, but also for his wife. She saw what God was doing. She hadn't abandoned her husband, but had stayed with him, and now saw God restoring double to them. They could truly say, "Oh taste and see that the LORD is good."

Job's livelihood returned with a vengeance so that now they had double the oxen, donkeys, sheep, and livestock. God gave them back ten more children—seven sons and three daughters—exactly the number they had before they lost everything.

These are the verses that opened up a different perspective to me concerning Job's wife. Job didn't marry another woman. He and his wife reconnected, not just spiritually and emotionally, but also physically. I'm sure their conversations concerned rebuilding, and starting a family of their own again. One of them might have said, "God gave us double of everything, but I don't want double the children; I just want the ten we had." They would have recovered intimacy in their relationship and they would have had to be healed to have ten more children at their age. Job or his wife might have said to each other, "Let's go make our family tonight! Tonight's gonna be a good night!" And so it was.

It is interesting that Scripture records the names of his daughters, but not the sons. Usually it gives lists of sons' names in genealogies and elsewhere, like in Mark 6:3. *"'Is this not the carpenter, the Son of Mary, and brother of James, Joses, Judas, and Simon? And are not His sisters here with us?' So they were offended at Him."*

Notice Mark lists the names of Jesus' brothers, and mentions His sisters, but with no names.

Here is another example: After the death of Abraham's wife Sarah, Abraham marries Keturah and has a family with her and names all the sons.

> *"And after this, Abraham buried Sarah his wife in the cave of the field of Machpelah, before Mamre (that is, Hebron) in the land of Canaan. So the field and the cave that is in it were deeded to Abraham by the sons of Heth as property for a burial place. Now Abraham was old, well advanced in age; and the LORD had blessed Abraham in all things"* (Genesis 23:19-24:1).

> *"Abraham again took a wife, and her name was Keturah. And she bore him Zimran, Jokshan, Medan, Midian, Ishbak, and Shuah. Jokshan begot Sheba and Dedan. And the sons of Dedan were Asshurim, Letushim, and Leummim. And the sons of Midian were Ephah, Epher, Hanoch, Abidah, and Eldaah. All these were the children of Keturah"* (Genesis 25:1-4).

Keturah means "perfumed; incense; a type of prayer."

Since Scripture doesn't record daughters' names generally, the Book of Job is different. The Book of Job mentions seven sons, but doesn't give their names. It mentions three daughters and names them all.

This fact caught my attention, and when I studied this line of thinking deeper, a picture developed, not through human reasoning, but through revelation from Heaven.

I found out that each name is significant, rich, and abundant in revelation. We will cover their meanings in the next chapter.

Our God is a God of Restoration!

"[The LORD, the Shepherd of His People: A Psalm of David:] The LORD is my shepherd; I shall not want. He makes me to lie down in green pastures; He leads me beside the still waters. He restores my soul; He leads me in the paths of righteousness For His name's sake" (Psalm 23:1-3).

After we've experienced the greatest test of our faith, or the most intense spiritual warfare; after the greatest of tragedies we may face in this life, may we never forget God wants to restore our lives! Declare this out loud:

God wants to restore my life!

Restore means, "He causes my life to be re-established."

"So I will restore to you the years that the swarming locust has eaten, the crawling locust, the consuming locust, and the chewing locust, my great army which I sent among you. You shall eat in plenty and be satisfied, and praise the name of the LORD your God, Who has dealt wondrously with you; and My people shall never be

put to shame. Then you shall know that I am in the midst of Israel: I am the LORD your God and there is no other. My people shall never be put to shame" (Joel 2:25-27).

Has a "locust" destroyed, devastated, paralyzed, or stopped your life? God wants to give you your life back. He is the God who Restores.

Is there a "locust" chewing away at your mind today—the "locust" of bitterness, unforgiveness, betrayal, or hurt? Locust of self-hatred, self-condemnation, anxiety, worry, or fear? Locust of anger, rage, or reaction? God is a restoring God and says to you today, "I will restore to you the years that the locusts have eaten." Notice the terms Scripture uses—"swarming, crawling, chewing, and consuming locust"—all these describe the work of SATAN in our lives sent to steal, kill, and destroy.

I have learned that, often, when we are at the end of our rope, stuck in a hopeless situation, in the darkest hour of our lives, that is when God shows up as our Restorer.

Once when David was coming home tired, weakened from a battle at Ziglag, he was faced with devastation:

"Now it happened, when David and his men came to Ziklag, on the third day, that the Amalekites had invaded the South and Ziklag, attacked Ziklag and burned it with fire, and had taken captive the women and those who were there, from small to great; they did not kill anyone, but carried them away and went their way. So David and his men came to the city, and there it was, burned with fire; and their wives, their sons, and their daughters had been taken captive. Then David and the people who were with him lifted up their voices and wept, until they had no more power to weep. And

> David's two wives, Ahinoam the Jezreelitess, and Abigail the widow of Nabal the Carmelite, had been taken captive. Now David was greatly distressed, for the people spoke of stoning him, because the soul of all the people was grieved, every man for his sons and his daughters. But David strengthened himself in the LORD his God. Then David said to Abiathar the priest, Ahimelech's son, 'Please bring the ephod here to me.' And Abiathar brought the ephod to David. So David inquired of the LORD, saying, 'Shall I pursue this troop? Shall I overtake them?' And He answered him, 'Pursue, for you shall surely overtake them and without fail recover all'" (1 Samuel 30:1-8).

"So David recovered all that the Amalekites had carried away, and David rescued his two wives. And nothing of theirs was lacking, either small or great, sons or daughters, spoil or anything which they had taken from them; David recovered all" (1 Samuel 30:18-19).

God did it for David; he recovered it all. He will do it for you. What has been ripped off in your life? What has been broken in your life? What is out of alignment in your life? He is the God who Restores.

Picture your life returning again. See yourself laughing, enjoying your spouse, loving your family, loving your job, church, and friends. Do you have children away from the Lord, out there caught in the world's web? They are returning home, they are turning back to their families; He is recovering it all.

It's time to look up and away from the thing that has distracted you from receiving your answer, your deliverance, and your freedom. It's time to look up and away from past failures, mistakes, and addictions, and break out today, for God is a restoring God.

My life seemed to be over nearly thirty-five years ago. Some people around rejoiced that Rick Ciaramitaro was knocked down and, they thought, out of the race. Some were happy that my life looked very broken, extremely hopeless, and incredibly painful, but God…!

Hear those words again: BUT GOD…!

The God who Restores, gave me back my life, my dignity, and His abundant favor. Today I can say confidently,

Don't give up!

It's not too late!

Don't throw in the towel, you're not a quitter, you're not gonna run away. There is another page to be written in your book—another script you can't see just yet, because He is the God who Restores. Breathe in those words, my friend. Dream again! Better days are ahead!

I can't say it enough: He is the God who Restores. Your life is coming back, my friend. It's already happening! Hope is arising inside you. Dreams are arising once again. Watch and see! You will rejoice as you say boldly, "He is the God who gave me my life back." This will be your testimony.

> *"For I will restore health unto thee, and I will heal thee of thy wounds, saith the LORD; because they called thee an Outcast, saying, This is Zion, whom no man seeketh after"* (Jeremiah 30:17, KJV).

Someone reading has been labeled by judgmental, critical, dispassionate brothers and sisters of the day as an *outcast*—one who has been rejected by home, family, society, church, or fellowship. One who feels like a vagabond wanderer without a place to call home, but the Lord who Restores says, "I will restore your health; I will heal your wounds."

When God gets done with you, your life will return. You will be one that says, "I have tasted and seen that the Lord is good." His goodness will lead you to repentance from your old ways. His Glory will restore you to wholeness, soundness of mind, healthy emotions, a healthy thought life, and a healthy body, because He is the God who Restores.

> "Restore unto me the joy of thy salvation; and uphold me with thy free spirit. Then will I teach transgressors thy way; and sinners shall be converted unto thee" (Psalm 51:12-13, KJV).

David's fellowship with God was broken, his countenance was downcast, his hopes were fading away, his peace was long-gone, yet he knew from where his restoration and life would be returned to him, and God did restore the joy of his salvation. God gave him new hope. God picked him up again, and David's life came back again.

Your life is coming back too. You are not too far gone. You haven't committed the "unpardonable sin." That is a lie the Enemy has embedded in your mind. You are not finished in life, but you are entering a new life, and new day.

Abraham was strong in faith, giving glory to God and thanking God. Stop for a moment now and thank God that you're getting back on track. The God who Restores is coming through for you. You are coming into the abundant life in Christ, my friend.

In the next chapter we will see how the God who Restores brought hope back to Job's wife, how her life changed, how she dreamed again, and saw the double-portion blessing come upon her and her husband. You will rejoice as we walk through the process of restoration in the life of this secret heroine.

CHAPTER FIVE

Job's Wife

I have been waiting to share the revelation in this chapter from the moment I wrote the Introduction. In the following text are three verses I would like to break down for you. Notice, they are right at the end of the Book of Job:

> "So Eliphaz the Temanite and Bildad the Shuhite and Zophar the Naamathite went and did as the LORD commanded them; for the LORD had accepted Job. And the LORD restored Job's losses when he prayed for his friends. Indeed the LORD gave Job twice as much as he had before. Then all his brothers, all his sisters, and all those who had been his acquaintances before, came to him and ate food with him in his house; and they consoled him and comforted him for all the adversity that the LORD had brought upon him. Each one gave him a piece of silver and each a ring of gold.
>
> "Now the LORD blessed the latter days of Job more than his beginning; for he had fourteen thousand sheep, six

thousand camels, one thousand yoke of oxen, and one thousand female donkeys. He also had seven sons and three daughters. And he called the name of the first Jemimah, the name of the second Keziah, and the name of the third Keren-Happuch. In all the land were found no women so beautiful as the daughters of Job; and their father gave them an inheritance among their brothers. After this Job lived one hundred and forty years, and saw his children and grandchildren for four generations. So Job died, old and full of days" (Job 42:9-17).

One of my favorite verses in the entire Book of Job is "Indeed the LORD gave Job twice as much as he had before" (Job 42:10). *Indeed* means "in fact, in reality, in truth, truly to confirm and amplify a previous statement."

Job obtained twice as much as he had had previously.

If we could just get a glimpse, when we are in the most dismal and seemingly defeated times of our lives, of what the other side of the storm looks like! On the other side there is a major promotion, blessing, breakthrough, freedom, answer to prayer, and restoration beyond our highest expectations.

On one side we experience total loss.

On the other side, total victory.

We move from shame, like Rahab in Joshua 2:1, to the Hall of Fame in Hebrews 11:31; from defeat to champion like Gideon in Judges 6:12—overcoming; from hopeless to hope. This is our God!

Next, these verses emphasize, *"Now the LORD blessed the latter days of Job more than his beginning"* (Job 42:12), yet in Job's darkest hour he mentioned wishing he had never even been born. God has a way of intervening in circumstances that are beyond our own reasoning and rational understanding; we just can't figure it out. It is totally supernatural in its origin and ways. *"Now to Him who is able to do exceedingly abundantly above all that we ask or think, according to the power that works in us, to Him be glory in the church by Christ Jesus to all generations, forever and ever. Amen"* (Ephesians 3:20-21).

I have recognized that on the other side of some of the greatest, hardest and most difficult situations we experience in life, there is a promotion, or breakthrough of some kind. The Bible is filled with stories that confirm this pattern. For example, Nebuchadnezzar is quoted as saying:

> *"Blessed be the God of Shadrach, Meshach, and Abed-Nego, who sent His Angel and delivered His servants who trusted in Him, and they have frustrated the king's word, and yielded their bodies, that they should not serve nor worship any god except their own God! Therefore I make a decree that any people, nation, or language which speaks anything amiss against the God of Shadrach, Meshach, and Abed-Nego shall be cut in pieces, and their houses shall be made an ash heap; because there is no other God who can deliver like this. Then the king promoted Shadrach, Meshach, and Abed-Nego in the province of Babylon"* (Daniel 3:28-30).

The three young men had to endure a severe test of faith. They had to overcome a powerful spirit of fear, but they received, for their faith, miraculous deliverance by the Angel of the Lord.

In the last part of the chapter we see the word *then*. Immediately after that test they heard the word *promotion*, which means "advancement in rank or position."

I remember my dad using the expression, "No pain, no gain." In life the greatest tests, challenges, or hardships we endure have a good ending on the other side for believers. For example, the Apostle Paul and all the men with him hadn't seen a reprieve in the weather out at sea for fourteen days. Then,

> "...as day was about to dawn, Paul implored them all to take food, saying, 'Today is the fourteenth day you have waited and continued without food, and eaten nothing. Therefore I urge you to take nourishment, for this is for your survival, since not a hair will fall from the head of any of you.' And when he had said these things, he took bread and gave thanks to God in the presence of them all; and when he had broken it he began to eat. Then they were all encouraged, and also took food themselves. And in all we were two hundred and seventy-six persons on the ship. So when they had eaten enough, they lightened the ship and threw out the wheat into the sea" (Acts 27:33-38).

The situation looked dismal. Paul broke bread, served communion, and gave thanks. The giving of thanks took place before deliverance came —another principle I learned from God's Word. Thanksgiving sanctifies the atmosphere for the mighty God to move into.

We read on to the close of Acts 27:

> "When it was day, they did not recognize the land; but they observed a bay with a beach, onto which they planned to run the ship if possible. And they let go the anchors and left them in the sea, meanwhile loosing the rudder ropes; and they hoisted the mainsail to the wind and made for shore. But striking a place where two seas

met, they ran the ship aground; and the prow stuck fast and remained immovable, but the stern was being broken up by the violence of the waves. And the soldiers' plan was to kill the prisoners, lest any of them should swim away and escape. But the centurion, wanting to save Paul, kept them from their purpose, and commanded that those who could swim should jump overboard first and get to land, and the rest, some on boards and some on parts of the ship. And so, it was that they all escaped safely to land" (Acts 27:39-44).

Here the death sentence was given to two hundred seventy-six people on the ship. They crashed into rocks. The ship broke up. The prisoners imagined it was the end of the line for them, but Paul had said not one would be harmed. While it seemed impossible, yet, in life, impossibilities for man are not impossibilities for God. Because of one man—Paul—they were all rescued. One man!

We read, *"...they all escaped safely to land."* How amazing! If we could just receive a revelation in the midst of our pain, suffering, challenging time, overwhelming circumstances, betrayal, rejection, down-and-out time, that God is there orchestrating a plan of promotion and advancement, ruling and reigning.

We see the reward of endurance in the stories of Joseph in Egypt, Daniel in the lions' den, Samson after he lost his eyes, King David, Nehemiah, and the list goes on and on. That is why Paul wrote,

"Do not be deceived, God is not mocked; for whatever a man sows, that he will also reap. For he who sows to his flesh will of the flesh reap corruption, but he who sows to the Spirit will of the Spirit reap everlasting life. And let

us not grow weary while doing good, for in due season we shall reap if we do not lose heart. Therefore, as we have opportunity, let us do good to all, especially to those who are of the household of faith" (Galatians 6:7-10).

Don't give up!
Don't quit!
Don't cave in!
Don't back down!
Persist!

Your deliverance is right at the end of the challenge. It's there for you to grab and hold onto. The last page of your life has not been written yet. There is a new day, new hope, new dream, and new victory, all on the other side of your most adverse situation.

God is faithful.
Trust Him today.
Don't lose faith.
Don't let discouragement overwhelm you.
Victory is yours.
Breakthrough is yours.
Promotion is yours.

Many years ago when my first wife divorced me, I was so discouraged. The harder I tried, the worse things got. Then I got a call from my former wife's attorney, suggesting the boys and I go for some psychological testing. I couldn't understand at the time why the divorce was happening, what I had done, and why I needed testing. These, along with many other questions bombarded my mind. Off we went to the psychological testing that was to last a week for each one of us. After a few hours, I was done and

I said, "But I was told it would be a week long?" She said, "You're finished," and proceeded to make appointments for the boys. The boys and I all finished up in less than a week. Then the ex-wife went for her testing. As a result, I received full custody of the boys. God's light overcame the darkness, but I had to submit to the testing first. We may not like the process, but we will like the end results if we stick with Jesus. Our darkest nights can become our brightest days if we don't become weary in well doing, for in due season we reap if we don't faint, according to God's Word.

Don't quit my friend! Better days are ahead. You will see breakthrough, and taste the experience that the Lord is good. His mercy is new every morning. Weeping may endure for the night, but joy comes in the morning.

Is this word for you? Know that joy is coming, and there is a morning after the storm. Sadness, brokenness, painfulness, and heaviness are leaving with it. Read Scripture and note the miracles recorded throughout the Bible. They are based on the principles we need to know, proclaim, and shout from the housetops: joy comes! A new day is dawning for you my friend, if you don't give up.

The good news doesn't end there. Another thing these verses in the Book of Job emphasize is that Job and his wife were blessed with fourteen thousand sheep, six thousand camels, one thousand yoke of oxen, and more. I am sure they were very excited and happy because their wealth doubled. But even more so, God restored their family and gave them ten more children: seven sons and three daughters.

The number seven is foundational to God's Word and is used 735 times in Scripture, with many other references to seventh and sevenfold. The *biblical number seven* means "completeness and perfection in both physical and spiritual realms."

Many references exist in the Bible that mention the number seven. For instance, the creation of all things took place in seven days, there are seven days in a week, the Bible was divided into seven divisions—the Law, the Prophets, the Psalms, the Gospels, the Epistles, Paul's Epistles, and the book of Revelation. The total number of originally-inspired books was forty-nine, or seven times seven, equalling forty-nine, representing the absolute perfection of the Word of God. There are seven seals, seven trumpet and seven bowl judgments in Revelation. And here in our text we see Job and his wife with seven sons.

What is most interesting about these verses, is that none of the sons are named. We saw that after Sarah's death Abraham and Keturah had sons, and they were mentioned by name:

"Abraham again took a wife, and her name was Keturah. And she bore him Zimran, Jokshan, Medan, Midian, Ishbak, and Shuah. Jokshan begot Sheba and Dedan. And the sons of Dedan were Asshurim, Letushim, and Leummim. And the sons of Midian were Ephah, Epher, Hanoch, Abidah, and Eldaah. All these were the children of Keturah" (Genesis 25:1-4).

The Gospel of Mark treats Jesus' siblings in a similar manner:

"Then He went out from there and came to His own country, and His disciples followed Him. And when the Sabbath had come, He began to teach in the synagogue. And many hearing Him were astonished, saying,

'Where did this Man get these things? And what wisdom is this which is given to Him, that such mighty works are performed by His hands! Is this not the carpenter, the Son of Mary, and brother of James, Joses, Judas, and Simon? And are not His sisters here with us?' So they were offended at Him" (Mark 6:1-3).

Jesus' brothers, whom Joseph and Mary conceived after His birth, are mentioned by name, but then the writer says, *"His sisters here with us."*

Interestingly, Scripture doesn't mention Job's wife's death, nor does it mention that she saw her children and grandchildren.

Since, throughout Scripture, it is quite common to mention the names of sons and not of daughters, why are Job's daughters named?

Why does Scripture focus on their three daughters, naming each one, and commenting on the three as being the most beautiful women in the land?

Why were the girls given the same inheritance as their brothers?

Not only this, but Job lived another one hundred and forty years after the ten children were born and saw his children and grandchildren to four generations. Job died old and full of days. What great restoration!

Unfortunately, we don't know the full extent of Job's wife's blessing. While both Job and his wife experienced restoration, she was the secret heroine of the Bible as all the attention and focus is upon Job, but she gave birth to another ten children.

Somewhere in the restoration process the souls of both Job and his wife were also restored. Both had spoken hurtful things to one another in the bitterness of times past, but something happened within them that caused them to move forward from pain and despair, to enjoy their latter years even more than their earlier ones. What happened to them that they could enjoy intimacy again and conceive ten more children? This, along with the mystery of Job's daughters' names, were questions I hoped to resolve.

The answer is actually quite simple. We think restoration takes place in the blink of an eye—in a moment of time—through the laying on of hands, and it could happen that way. We think trauma of the soul can be healed suddenly, but, in most cases, I have come to realize that restoration is a process. It takes time, encouragement, and comfort for hope to come back into our lives. The following things bitter people usually cannot do:

- Job's wife did not abandon her husband.
- She stayed with him during the nine months of pain, suffering, and loss.
- She made love to her husband.

Bitter people tend to withdraw from their closest loved ones. How can we understand what happened? Two things are important.

First, the daughter's names are key. Each name is part of the process that Job and his wife worked through to rebuild their lives together. In Old Testament times, a name was more than just an identification tag. It revealed a circumstance going on in a person's life, or the deepest intentions of the parents for their children.

Second, these three daughters were the most beautiful in all the land. How beautiful must they have been when born? There weren't any blemishes on their faces. They possessed qualities that gave great delight, or satisfaction to the senses and the mind. Excellent in its kind, is the description Scripture gives of all three daughters.

Prior to when my wife and I had our son Timothy, we thought our newest addition was going to be a daughter. In those days we didn't have ultrasound and tests that could identify a child's sex. We had picked many female names and no male names because we absolutely believed he would be a she. After he was born, I told the doctor to give me a day to choose a boy's name. I visited with my wife and newborn son and went home to read my Bible.

I happened to be reading 1 and 2 Timothy. As always, I expected the Holy Spirit to share something with me in God's Word. Nothing was standing out to me, but I felt compelled to keep reading those two books. Suddenly, I heard the Holy Spirit say, "Name your son Timothy. Timothy means to honour or reverence God, and every time you see your son, he will be a reminder for you to honour the Lord."

To this very day, it is so.

Historically, children were occasionally named after an event, or something of importance in the family's life. The name *Moses*, for instance, means "drawn out of the water." The name *Edom* means "red." The Hebrews also named their children after something God had done in their lives. For instance, *Emmanuel* means "God with us," and *David* means "beloved."

One of my highlights in pastoring, has been dedicating children to the Lord in special services. For my African brothers and sisters, names are very important at baby dedications. Most choose names that reference God in some way: God has blessed; God has delighted; God has favoured us, and so on. How precious and honouring!

There is something very powerful about the names we will examine in the study of Job's wife. Let's look again at the biblical passage:

> "He also had seven sons and three daughters. And he called the name of the first Jemimah, the name of the second Keziah, and the name of the third Keren-Happuch. In all the land were found no women so beautiful as the daughters of Job; and their father gave them an inheritance among their brothers. After this Job lived one hundred and forty years, and saw his children and grandchildren for four generations. So Job died, old and full of days" (Job 42:13-17).

We will now look at how the daughters' names offer keys to part of the process that Job and his wife experienced as they rebuilt their lives together.

CHAPTER SIX

Jemimah—One Day at a Time

The name of their first daughter, *Jemimah*, according to *Strong's Dictionary of OT Words*, means "warm and affectionate." It also means "dove" and "day by day."

The word *warm* suggests "animated, lively, brisk, or vigorous," as well as "close to something sought." This tells us little Jemimah may have been lively, full of life, and very close to her Mom and Dad. She likely was affectionately, fondly, tenderly, and warmly embraced and attached.

What a great description of the incredible, irreplaceable bond between father/daughter and mother/daughter, as well as Dad and Mom together with their little daughter! Warmth and affection between Job and his wife would have kicked into high gear again. Their chemistry had never left, but their emotions had been damaged from the tragedy, and now, in naming their child, we see their feelings were returning.

"Dove" was another meaning attached to the name *Jemimah*. It references a pure white member of the dove species used as a symbol of innocence, gentleness, tenderness, and peace. Thus little Jemimah was pure and innocent and her name describes the peace that Job and his wife had found once again.

We have six children. While they were growing up, every Father's Day, birthday, and Christmas the children would ask me, "Dad, what can we get you for the special day?" My answer was quick, consistent, and repeated often, year after year: "Peace in the house!" Now they are married, and understand the value of having peace between one another.

It may have taken a while for Job and his wife to get their peace back, but when Jemimah came along, it happened, and she reminded them of it. *Jemimah* means "day by day." When I saw those words, they leaped off the page as I studied this, and it came to me that, after a hit—major adversity, disastrous experience, tragedy, disappointment—the best advice I can give you from God's Word is to take it one day at a time.

Day by day we get better.
Day by day we get through.
Day by day we start moving ahead and healing.

The most important thing is that day by day we move ahead, get out of the ruts in life—the painful memories that we have rehearsed over and over again in our minds. We should only look back to forgive those who caused us the deepest pain—those who betrayed us, took advantage of us, broke their vows. Progress happens day by day.

Listen carefully: restoration is a process. Don't expect a quick fix, especially when your emotions are deeply damaged. It takes time. People who know me may consider me a rather positive, grateful, and steady person, but I must admit, at times I struggle with wanting to run and move far away from everybody to the Northwest Territories. It's like David said, *"Oh, that I had wings like a dove! I would fly away and be at rest. Indeed, I would wander far off, and remain in the wilderness. Selah. I would hasten my escape from the windy storm and tempest"* (Psalm 55:6-8).

"I want to fly away" might be a common theme when we are faced with debilitating circumstances. Maybe that's why teaching on the Rapture is so popular today.

We've all had days when pain we suffer from injustices and betrayals is so intense that we can hardly get out of bed. On those days we just want to isolate ourselves; but those are days wasted rehearsing circumstances in our minds, trying to make sense of things that don't make sense. As they say, "No rhyme or reason to it."

On those days we don't even want to try. We just want to give up. We struggle to pray. We don't want to feel. Our situation seems so demoralizing, frustrating, and discouraging that our only recourse in the end is taking it one day at a time.

This is the beginning of restoration—keep our hearts warm and affectionate, and take one day, not two, but one day at a time, as the writer of Ecclesiastes said: *"[Everything has its time.] To everything there is a season; a time for every purpose under heaven"* (Ecclesiastes 3:1).

After the toughest of blows in life we need to take it one day at a time to get built back up again, to regroup, to dream again, and to encourage ourselves in the Lord. This is the antidote to impatience and former frustrations. Shutting off the many voices in our minds from the past, can only be done that way.

Today psychologists have diagnosed many in our society with Post Traumatic Stress Disorder (PTSD). They have become deeply stuck in life's ruts, and as a result they may become quite irritable, or short-fused, and really struggle with trust, especially when it involves a betrayal. The betrayal of a relationship, and then divorce, can paralyze the victims for decades, and as part of the recovery process they may have to take two steps forward and one back, yet they are still gaining and moving ahead.

Jemimah means "day by day." In this process, triggers are disarmed, the pain begins to decrease slowly, joy and laughter gradually return, the countenance begins to relax, and smiles appear as the peace of God floods the heart, and warmth and affection return.

Job and his wife had a severe case of PTSD, as we know it today, but holding their new baby and smiling at her was part of their recovery process.

I so appreciate my friends Pastor Brian Danter and Pastor Luc LeBoeuf, who walked with me day by day after the abandonment and betrayal I personally experienced. I had a few good days, but mostly challenging ones, yet over time and after many mistakes and triggered reactions that I am not proud of, I began to heal. I recognized that restoration is a process to be taken one day at a time, and to use those words is not a mere cliché. It is a decision to get up and start every day with a few small steps forward. Always moving forward, looking up; looking ahead, not behind.

I want to encourage you today: If you are struggling with an addiction, stuck in a rut, wounded deeply, traumatized, or stuck, it's time to reach out to those around you who have offered help. Let them pray with you, encourage you, and walk with you through the process of restoration.

We can't do it on our own, my friend. We all need the Jemimahs of our day in our lives. Don't keep anxiety stuffed down inside of you. Get rid of anger and rage, and put an end to the cycle of abuse with which you have tormented your mind day after day. Instead, day after day, start speaking to the dry bones.

> Speak life to your soul.
> Speak life to your body.
> Speak life to those who wounded you.

Say out loud: I release you and let you go; I forgive you. I'm moving forward from this rut, this addiction, this painful experience.

Deprogram the negative emotions and reprogram yourself with God's Word:

> *"Therefore do not cast away your confidence, which has great reward. For you have need of endurance, so that after you have done the will of God, you may receive the promise: 'For yet a little while, and He who is coming will come and will not tarry. Now the just shall live by faith; but if anyone draws back, My soul has no pleasure in him.' But we are not of those who draw back to perdition, but of those who believe to the saving of the soul"* (Hebrews 10:35-39).

Jemimah reminds each of us to take one step at a time, day by day, until we get better and no longer are in bitterness. To the New Testament Church, the Body of Christ, the Apostle Paul gave very specific instructions on what to do: *"Let all bitterness, wrath, anger, clamor, and evil speaking be put away from you, with all malice. And be kind to one another, tenderhearted, forgiving one another, even as God in Christ forgave you"* (Ephesians 4:31-32).

Every day that I was stuck in the past, I daily had to get rid of bitterness, wrath, anger, clamour—the things that incited uproar and evil speaking. I had to rid myself of malice, which is a desire to inflict injury, harm, or suffering on another, either because of a hostile impulse, or out of deep-seated meanness.

When we are abused, traumatized, paralyzed, or crippled emotionally, we want the people who did this to us "to pay." We want them injured, and we can become quite hostile, but God says, "Put it away. Don't entertain it, dwell on it, or nurse it. Don't rehearse it and don't dig a deeper pit, but day by day come out of it."

Start today to speak blessings over your mind, will, emotions, body, friends, family, relationships, and health. Speak favour over your circumstances and damaged emotions, and speak forgiveness toward your enemies. Cancel all debts of unforgiveness today. These are steps of your day by day process to healing. Never forget these words: *"Now may the God of peace Himself sanctify you completely; and may your whole spirit, soul, and body be preserved blameless at the coming of our LORD Jesus Christ. He who calls you is faithful, who also will do it"* (1 Thessalonians 5:23-24). God, who is faithful, trustworthy, reliable, sure, steadfast, and dependable, will do it. Believe it today, and the process of restoration will begin in your life, my friend.

It's going to be a good day! You're getting up! You're getting out of the ruts of life, and your restoration has begun.

Many years ago, my earthly mother took sick and was on many medications, and the doctor put her in a hospice-type facility to die. She was a very strong woman and always dressed prim and proper. Cathy and I went to visit her shortly after her placement. When I entered the room, I was shocked at the change: she was very frail, drugged up, and so weak that she kept dozing off. I walked out and wept seeing her that way. Cathy brought me back in to say goodbye. When I leaned over her to kiss her goodbye, she grabbed me and said, "I want you to know, Richard, I'm not dying in this place, but I'm getting off all these drugs and getting out of here." Then she dozed off again. I don't recommend in any way that people get off their medications "without medical supervision," so please don't use this story for that purpose. See your doctor for their advice before making any changes to your medications.

Day by day, my mother got off the medications, started eating again, and day by day became stronger and healthier until life returned. She walked out of that place a few weeks later restored, and lived many more years.

My admonition to all of us is this: start now, and speak life back into your soul. Take it one day at a time, but focus forward, not backward; move ahead, not behind.

One day at a time is the way Job's wife did it. She started getting back to normal again—dreaming, making progress—and lived a journey of faith that encourages us all today. According to Isaiah, *"Do not remember the former things, nor consider the things of old. Behold, I will do a new thing, now it shall spring forth; shall you not know it? I will even make a road in the wilderness and rivers in the desert"* (Isaiah 43:18-19).

In the movie *Amish Grace*, the mother whose daughter was murdered, had to forgive the murderer every day, over and over again, until she eventually began to feel better. I can say today that, by God's grace, I have forgiven my enemies, betrayers, and those who caused me great pain. Sometimes I had to forgive seventy-times-seven times every day, or four hundred ninety times a day, but I kept at it day by day, and by the mercy of that grace, the Word clicked inside me and I was released. May we all live day by day, in kindness and affection by applying Philippians 3:13-14: *"Brethren I do not count myself to have apprehended; but one thing I do, forgetting those things which are behind and reaching forward to those things which are ahead, I press toward the goal for the prize of the upward call of God in Christ Jesus."*

Similarly, day by day, Job's wife had to get back up and overcome, until she conceived ten more children and lived a long, full life with her family: *"After this Job lived one hundred and forty years, and saw his children and grandchildren for four generations"* (Job 42:16).

In the next chapter we will see how the second sister, Keziah, represents the next step to restoration.

CHAPTER SEVEN

Keziah—A Sweet Aroma

"*And he called the name of the first Jemimah, the name of the second Keziah, and the name of the third Keren-Happuch. In all the land were found no women so beautiful as the daughters of Job; and their father gave them an inheritance among their brothers*" (Job 42:14-15).

Job's second daughter was named *Keziah*, which is taken from the Hebrew word meaning "*cassia* or cinnamon"—the name of a spice tree.

Cassia is Chinese cinnamon—an aromatic spice, meaning "having an aroma." The words "having an aroma" stood out to me, concerning the name *Keziah*, which, according to *The Free Dictionary* by Farley and *Strong's Dictionary of OT Words*, means "having a distinctive odor by which a person or animal can be traced; the sense of smell; an instinctive ability for finding out or detecting." I immediately connected it with Paul's words in 2 Corinthians:

"For we are to God the fragrance of Christ among those who are being saved and among those who are perishing. To the one we are the aroma of death leading to death, and to the other the aroma of life leading to life. And who is sufficient for these things?" (2 Corinthians 2:15-16).

By naming their daughter Keziah, Job and his wife declared that a new season had come into their lives—a different atmosphere. No longer were they suffering the negativity, or murmuring of *"curse God and die,"* or the "woe-is-me" pity parties, but they were now enjoying a sweet aroma of gratitude and praise.

Our aromas attract either good or bad to us. They attract either the Holy Spirit, or demonic power into our lives. Murmuring and complaining is a scent or aroma that attracts the demonic, and praise and thanksgiving attracts the Presence of God to our lives. I have many bottles of cologne that have been given to me over the years as gifts. There is one scent that I spray on that attracts Cathy to me. She says, "I love that smell." The naming of Keziah was an aroma that attracts the Presence of God, and it's simply called "Gratitude."

Many years ago, my friend Mauro Girgenti and I were driving to Venice, Italy, and his wife, Connie, and Cathy were in the back seat of the car chatting. Before we had set out, I had stopped at the grocery store to pick up a jar of anchovies and some fresh *ciabatta* bread. In the front seat the two Italian guys were ripping apart the bread and placing anchovies on it. The "aroma" of anchovies filled the atmosphere and reached the back seat. The girls started gagging.

"Roll down the windows!" they cried. "That's disgusting! How can you eat that stuff?"

We were thoroughly enjoying every bite, but the aroma of anchovies attracted a strong reaction from our wives. You might say, to Mauro and me, anchovies were an aroma of life, whereas to our wives they were an aroma of disgust. The name *Keziah* reminds us of the aroma that attracts God to our lives—gratitude. Job and his wife began to praise and thank God, and shifted the aroma of death off their lives, off their marriage, and off their future. The naming of Keziah was a declaration of the sweet-smelling aroma of gratitude ascending up to God.

After we start our journey of restoration one day at a time, day by day, we travel on a new pathway of gratitude—one of thanking God for what we have, not complaining to Him about what we don't have. We become appreciative for the small things in life, as we walk the pathway to better and greater things ahead of us. Keziah, like Paul, began to understand the power of aromas and the attraction they have: *"Therefore be imitators of God as dear children. And walk in love, as Christ also has loved us and given Himself for us, an offering and a sacrifice to God for a sweet-smelling aroma"* (Ephesians 5:1-2).

Has it occurred to you that forgiveness is an aroma that attracts God to your life, while unforgiveness attracts the demonic?

Have you considered that fear attracts the Devil to our lives, while faith attracts God?

Job and his wife attracted God to their lives by the aroma of thanksgiving, and now dispersed a sweet aroma before the Lord. Both Job and his wife began to appreciate what remained between them. Their focus changed from dwelling on the past, to looking forward to their future with God.

For all of us, Satan, the god of this world, has strategized an evil day. Often he has planned for many years how to take us out, how to steal, kill and ultimately destroy our lives. When Job and his wife named their daughter Keziah, it changed the playing field, spiritually, by taking power away from Satan to afflict them and transferring power to God to bless them.

When we come to one another in a spirit of true humility and grace, and acknowledge our pain, frustrations, and hurts before God, asking Him to change us from whiners to winners, from throwing pity parties to rejoicing at Holy Spirit breakthroughs, something changes in the atmosphere. Heaven opens up and comes to earth. A portal opens for angels to travel back and forth and bring answers, deliverance, and freedom to our souls. Job and his wife got hold of the sweet aroma of praise and thanksgiving that activated Heaven's agenda, and turned their lives around to become productive, fruitful, and overcoming.

In the Old Testament, the Israelites made a voluntary, sweet-savour offering to the Lord, not to atone for sin, guilt, or wrongdoing, but out of a thankful heart. It was an offering that greatly delighted God then, as well as today. The New Testament writer says it well in Hebrews: *"Therefore by Him let us continually offer the sacrifice of praise to God, that is, the fruit of our lips, giving thanks to His name. But do not forget to do good and to share, for with such sacrifices God is well pleased"* (Hebrews 13:15-16).

Gratitude was the sacrifice Job and his wife brought to the Lord in the naming of Keziah; they may not have felt like it; they might not have been up to it, but they brought it anyway, and God came through for them with a big "YES," giving them double for all their trouble and ten more children. Hallelujah! This was a restoration that caused their lives to return once again.

In the spiritual realm, sweet smelling aromas of gratitude attract the presence of God to us. Jonah's deliverance came when the aroma went up: *"'But I will sacrifice to You with the voice of thanksgiving; I will pay what I have vowed. Salvation is of the LORD.' So the LORD spoke to the fish, and it vomited Jonah onto dry land"* (Jonah 2:9-10).

Is it possible Jonah would have died if he hadn't brought the "voice of the sacrifice of thanksgiving?" Notice how quickly his deliverance came after he voiced his thanksgiving.

Perhaps you need a manifestation of the power of God through deliverance. God is waiting for a sacrifice from you. He is waiting for you to voice thanksgiving so He can bring your freedom. Thank Him right where you are now and watch the atmosphere of heaviness, oppression, and fear shift off your life, my friend. When you praise with a voice of thanksgiving, you are doing battle. That is how we fight in the spirit realm.

The positive aromas of love, patience, goodness, generosity, forgiveness, and kindness attract the presence of God to us. Scents or aromas of strife, arguing, division, jealousy, rage, and disunity are aromas that attract the demonic into the atmosphere of our marriages, families, homes, workplaces, and even churches.

We have looked at the meaning of the word *cassia* with respect to Keziah's name. Now let's look at the word *cinnamon*. It has many meanings that are spiritually applicable.

In Job's day, just as today, cinnamon has definite health benefits. It has anti-inflammatory properties that can help relieve arthritic pain and stiffness in joints and muscles.

Keziah (cinnamon), therefore, reminds us not to get into pride, and not to be stiff-necked and rebellious, but to stay humble before God and one another.

Humility, fueled by thanksgiving, is the springboard to restoration of our souls.

Here are ten health benefits of cinnamon that are supported by scientific research:

1. Cinnamon is high in a substance with powerful medicinal properties.
2. Cinnamon is loaded with antioxidants.
3. Cinnamon has anti-inflammatory properties.
4. Cinnamon may cut the risk of heart disease.
5. Cinnamon can improve sensitivity to the hormone insulin.
6. Cinnamon lowers blood sugar levels and has a powerful anti-diabetic effect.
7. Cinnamon may have beneficial effects on neurodegenerative diseases.
8. Cinnamon may protect against cancer.
9. Cinnamon helps fight bacterial and fungal infections.
10. Cinnamon may help fight HIV.

Source: www.healthline.com/nutrition/10-proven-benefits-of-cinnamon

The aroma of cinnamon is calming and can also remind you to give your heavy burdens, cares, and weights that hinder, to the Lord, and to complete the race with faith.

One more meaning of *Keziah*, or *Cassia*, is "powdered bark," and it reveals more concerning this child's name.

Bark is hard and very tough, and after going through the trials and challenges of life, we can become either powdered, or soft inside, if we trust God, or we become even harder if we remain bitter or unforgiving. Let's stay soft no matter what life brings. Let's stay sweet in spite of the sour that hits our lives. I believe this parallels Job's wife who had to have started life from the inside out, and even though she may have had layer upon layer on the outside, like the layers of an onion, life returned from the inside as the aroma of praise and thanks went up.

My wife's former TV program was called *Life Inside Out*. Cathy named the program because of the importance of living life from the inside out. Religion tries to change folks from the outside in, but Christ changes us from the inside out. Similarly, the sweet aroma produced from inside Job's wife's heart, became her protection on the outside to continue her process of restoration.

For Job and his wife, the naming of Keziah was a major part of their restoration, just like thanksgiving will be a major part of your restoration and cause your life to be re-established once again. If you have been struggling in the ruts of life, murmuring, complaining, and wallowing in discontent, think on Keziah and shift negativity out of your life. Take daily doses of gratitude. Thank God for your spouse, children, family, friends, neighbours, and the precious folks in your life. Thank God for your place of employment, employers, and employees, and watch the atmosphere shift. May Keziah be a reminder to you and an invitation into a restored life:

> "And the LORD restored Job's losses when he prayed for his friends. Indeed the LORD gave Job twice as much as he had before" (Job 42:10).

"Restore to me the joy of Your salvation, and uphold me by Your generous Spirit" (Psalm 51:12).

"Restore us, O LORD God of hosts; cause Your face to shine, and we shall be saved!" (Psalm 80:19).

Saved means "to be open, wide or free, to be safe, deliver(-er), help, preserve, rescued, get victory" (Strong's Dictionary of OT Words).

May each of us reading about Keziah be reminded that God is awesome, amazing, all powerful, all knowing, and all seeing.

May each of us daily create an atmosphere for the presence of God to invade every area of our souls and heal and restore the broken-hearted.

May great restoration of damaged emotional wounds come, and may we be delivered and released of their assignments from our lives, in Jesus' Name.

May each of us reading this have our life returned to us—the life that is pleasing in God's sight.

In the final chapter we will read of the youngest of the three sisters, named Keren-Happuch. What a wonderful name this was for Job and his wife to choose!

CHAPTER EIGHT

Keren-Happuch—Rise Up and Be Restored

"Now the LORD blessed the latter days of Job more than his beginning; for he had fourteen thousand sheep, six thousand camels, one thousand yoke of oxen, and one thousand female donkeys. He also had seven sons and three daughters. And he called the name of the first Jemimah, the name of the second Keziah, and the name of the third Keren-Happuch. In all the land were found no women so beautiful as the daughters of Job; and their father gave them an inheritance among their brothers. After this Job lived one hundred and forty years, and saw his children and grandchildren for four generations. So Job died, old and full of days" (Job 42:12-17).

Now we come to the end of the story about Job's wife, the secret heroine of the Bible. It concerns the youngest of the three daughters named *Keren-Happuch*. This name has several meanings, and each one is rich with revelation knowledge. *Strong's Dictionary of OT Words* defines *Keren-Happuch* as: "horn of cosmetic; horn of antimony." The term comes from two root words: "*qeren*—a horn or flask; a ray of light" and "*puk*—to paint; dye for the eyes, fair colours, glistering paint."

To the Orientals of that day, and to many in our day, it refers to "putting on face paint, or make up, around the edges of the eyelids to make the eyes look larger and have luster and look shining, brilliant, splendid, gorgeous, distinguished, strikingly admirable, or fine in appearance." These definitions imply action.

From these definitions we ascertain why Job and his wife named their third daughter *Keron-Happuch*. It's evident that Job's wife—after taking one day at a time, "day by day," to recover (noted in the name *Jemimah*), and after recovering praise and thanksgiving that rose to the Lord like a sweet aroma (evidenced by the name *Keziah*)—had now begun to take care of herself once again, to dress up elegantly, put on make-up, and look good for her husband. Job's wife hadn't parked in the pain and regrets of her past mistakes. Nor was she living a defeated life any longer. Instead she was rising up, shaking off depression, shaking off past defeats, breaking off chains of traumatic experiences, and adorning herself for her husband and God. She was dressing up and looking mighty fine again. She had pulled her old cosmetic box out of the closet, dusted it off, and started painting her eyelids, becoming radiant, shining, and beautiful. What followed from there? The fruits of coming together in the "tent of meeting" to have more children.

They obviously had an active, intimate life together once again. This tells us that the secret heroine of the Bible refused to stay down, defeated, overwhelmed, traumatized, bitter, angry, and so on, and that she got back up again. *"For a righteous man may fall seven times and rise again, but the wicked shall fall by calamity"* (Proverbs 24:16).

Job's wife was knocked down, but she had the will and fortitude to get back up again. That is a mark of heroes, the lifestyle of heroes. They take hits in life, but they don't give up. They kept moving forward; they began again to thank and praise God in every circumstance; they changed the atmosphere, and dressed for battle.

The Apostle Paul operated in this same spirit when life thrust its ugly blows at him:

> *"[Cast down but unconquered.] But we have this treasure in earthen vessels, that the excellence of the power may be of God and not of us. We are hard-pressed on every side, yet not crushed; we are perplexed, but not in despair; persecuted, but not forsaken; struck down, but not destroyed—always carrying about in the body the dying of the LORD Jesus, that the life of Jesus also may be manifested in our body"* (2 Corinthians 4:7-10).

Noteworthy, is also the fact that Job and his wife never divorced, or even separated, but remained together to have ten more children; I guess we could say in their marriage vows "for better or for worse, in sickness and in health."

Biblically, the number ten is symbolic of perfection, harmony, and Creation, and is connected to man following God's laws. Remember the Ten Commandments? In the Book of Genesis, the book of divine origins, *"God said"* occurs ten times. Having the numeric value, "ten" children was symbolic of perfection and harmony. Job and his wife got back into harmony and their Integrity stood the test of time.

In life and ministry, my wife and I have been knocked down many times, but we didn't stay down. We arose and got back up. We have learned that adversity is often the doorway into the greatest opportunities. We have learned that the greater the battles, the greater the hits, the severest spiritual attacks are all confirmation that the greatest breakthroughs are on the way. They point to the greatest victories ahead.

Look at adversity as an opportunity. Opportunity is there, but often disguised as adversity. Job's wife recognized that the Enemy brought genuine crisis to their lives and marriage, but God used her adversity and recovery as an instruction manual for us today on how to deal with crisis, contradictions, ruts in life, defeats, and how to recover all and get back up in life.

This secret heroine of faith had to push forward in spite of her damaged emotions and wounded heart. She had to get out her cosmetic box and take action. Action is a choice we all have to take at one time or another in our lives. I'm convinced that many people quit too soon. They give in and give up, and often their breakthroughs were just ahead of them on the next page of their journals—in the next season of their lives.

To all those crushed by adversity, addictions, betrayals, broken heartedness, failures, defeat from the past, I say, "RISE UP! You can do it! God believes in you!" I'm writing this to you, my friends, to encourage you to rise up.

Rise up from sitting around being depressed. Get out of bed today. Get up from past defeat. Spring up and again put on the armour of God as stated in Ephesians 6:10-16. God says He is causing your life to return again. Start speaking life, decreeing life, seeing and enjoying life again. Don't settle in and say, "My life is ruined; it's too late; it's not going to change; I'm too far gone." No! Fill the atmosphere with thanksgiving and songs of victory. Speak life over your health, your emotions, your dry season, and watch God arise in your life as your enemies are scattered.

Have you been listening to the Enemy's lies for way too long? Has he been telling you that you're nothing? That you're a loser? That's a lie! A blatant lie, my friend!

When your Mom and Dad conceived you, a billion sperm cells were in the running to make you, and only one was victorious. That one is in your DNA; you were conceived to be a champion, overcomer, victor, winner, and giant-slayer. That's who you are!

Victory is yours now. Believe it, speak it, and see it come to pass in your life.

Job's wife, in the opinion of many, was and is the greatest failure, the most insensitive, mean woman in the Bible, but not in God's eyes, or my eyes. She is a true heroine of faith to me. She is an example of a champion who got wounded in battle, but went back into the battle of life and won the victory.

What about you, my friend? Will you accept the lies of the Enemy of your soul as the final say, or will you change the atmosphere to line up with what God says? The choice is in your mouth: *"Death and life are in the power of the tongue, and those who love it will eat its fruit"* (Proverbs 18:21).

There remains yet another definition of the name *Keren-Happuch* for us to consider. The name also means "horn of antimony," or "lustrous and shining."

Notice the word *horn*. It is often used to signify strength and honour, because horns are the chief weapons and ornaments of the animals that possess them. They represent victory to the animal.

I have several rams' horns in my home and they remind me of victories to come. They are a reminder of aggressive strength inside each one of us. Horns are ornamental, but they are intended for battle. Job's wife used the horn of shining luster to battle the lies and temptations the evil one sent against her mind, marriage, and family.

The final question to each of us is, "What are you doing with your 'horns'—the aggressive nature and strength inside you?" Are you using your strength to resist the Enemy's lies and strongholds that affect your thoughts, or are you doing what Job's wife did – rising up and taking charge, day by day, creating a sweet aroma that changes the atmosphere? Are you applying "face paint" and "dressing for war" not against one another, but against the Enemy of our souls? The choice is yours, my friend. Let's watch and see your life return back to you again. Let's act on this instruction from the Lord:

> *"Therefore humble yourselves under the mighty hand of God, that He may exalt you in due time, casting all your care upon Him, for He cares for you. Be sober, be vigilant; because your adversary the devil walks about like a roaring lion, seeking whom he may devour. Resist him, steadfast in the faith, knowing that the same sufferings are experienced by your brotherhood in the world. But may the God of all grace, who called us to His eternal glory by Christ Jesus, after you have suffered a while, perfect, establish, strengthen, and settle you. To Him be the glory and the dominion forever and ever. Amen"* (1 Peter 5:6-11).

Job's wife didn't get the victory of restoration immediately, but she left an example of hope, encouragement, and strength for us to follow. May we never forget the end of her story! Read it again, because God is restoring your life, my friend, and causing it to return again:

> *"And the LORD restored Job's losses when he prayed for his friends. Indeed the LORD gave Job twice as much as he had before. Then all his brothers, all his sisters, and all those who had been his acquaintances before, came to him and ate food with him in his house; and they consoled him and comforted him for all the adversity that the LORD had brought upon him. Each one gave him a piece of silver and each a ring of gold.*
>
> *"Now the LORD blessed the latter days of Job more than his beginning; for he had fourteen thousand sheep, six thousand camels, one thousand yoke of oxen, and one thousand female donkeys. He also had seven sons and three daughters. And he called the name of the first Jemimah, the name of the second Keziah, and the name of the third Keren-Happuch. In all the land were found no women so beautiful as the daughters of Job; and their father gave them an inheritance among their brothers.*
> *"After this Job lived one hundred and forty years, and saw his children and grandchildren for four generations"* (Job 42:10-16).

Thirty-five years ago my life fell apart. I was devastated by abandonment and a divorce that greatly changed my life. I was discouraged—to many, I was a write-off, loser, and failure. But the God who restores our lives came on the scene. I received double for all the trouble I had experienced and am so thankful to the God who Restores.

The time to put the excuses aside is now; excuses are a language of defeated ones, but that's not you; you're a champion, a giant slayer, and you're seizing the opportunity for a decisive victory ahead of you.

This is your future too, my friend. Seize the opportunities to shift the atmosphere of your life to one of gratitude and watch your life return. It's your time now, my friend.

Rise up today.
Resist the Enemy of your soul.
Rejoice as victory manifests in your life.
May your life demonstrate to your future generations the God who Restores.

CPSIA information can be obtained
at www.ICGtesting.com
Printed in the USA
BVHW080947010921
615642BV00005B/8